HOW TO THINK
BIGGER

T0151143

Also by Mark Victor Hansen

BOOKS

Chicken Soup for the Soul series—254 different books in print

The One Minute Millionaire

Cracking the Millionaire Code

Cash in a Flash

How to Make the Rest of Your Life the Best of Your Life

The Aladdin Factor

Dare to Win

The Richest Kids in America

The Miracle of Tithing

The Power of Focus

The Miracles in You

Out of the Blue

Master Motivator

You Are the Solution

You Have a Book in You

Speed Write Your Personal Life Story

Speed Write Your First Fiction Book

Speed Write Your Nonfiction Book

Speed Write Your Mega Book Marketing Plan

Speed Write Your First Screenplay

Speed Write (and Deliver) Your Killer Speech

Speed Write Your Amazing Publishing Plan

Speed Edit Your First Book

Visualizing Is Realizing

Dreams Don't Have Deadlines

AUDIOS

How to Think Bigger than You Ever Thought You Could Think

Dreams Don't Have Deadlines

Visualizing Is Realizing

Sell Yourself Rich

Chicken Soup for the Soul series

The One Minute Millionaire

Cracking the Millionaire Code

HOW TO THINK
BIGGER

AND GO FROM ORDINARY . . .
TO EXTRAORDINARY

MARK VICTOR HANSEN

MEDIA

Published 2021 by Gildan Media LLC
aka G&D Media
www.GandDmedia.com

HOW TO THINK BIGGER. Copyright © 2021 Mark Victor Hansen. All rights reserved.

No part of this book may be used, reproduced or transmitted in any manner whatsoever, by any means (electronic, photocopying, recording, or otherwise), without the prior written permission of the author, except in the case of brief quotations embodied in critical articles and reviews. No liability is assumed with respect to the use of the information contained within. Although every precaution has been taken, the author and publisher assume no liability for errors or omissions. Neither is any liability assumed for damages resulting from the use of the information contained herein.

Front cover design by David Rheinhardt of Pyrographx

Interior design by Meghan Day Healey of Story Horse, LLC

Library of Congress Cataloging-in-Publication Data is available upon request

ISBN: 978-1-7225-0359-8

10   9   8   7   6   5   4   3   2   1

Contents

Contents

Foreword

Imagine your life filled with everything you wish for. Imagine every moment filled with awesome power. Imagine all your relationships being wonderful and your heart truly filled with happiness. Imagine fulfilling your purpose in life and being on track with your true destiny. Imagine the power of thinking bigger than you ever thought you could.

Mark Victor Hansen, master motivator, speaker, visionary, and cocreator of the Chicken Soup for the Soul empire, can show you how to achieve every dream you ever thought possible. In this book, Mark will teach you how to look at the world with different eyes—eyes of power, eyes of wisdom, eyes of prestige and passion. You'll see opportunities you never knew existed.

Mark will show you how to embrace every challenge and catapult yourself beyond your wildest dreams. He will show you how to eliminate fear and unhappiness from your life, along with everything that's holding you back from achieving the health and affluence that you desire and deserve. You'll have the power to make a difference in your own life and the lives of countless others.

In this book, Mark gives you proven techniques and secrets for discovering the genius within you. He'll teach you how to network and develop your own dream team to establish relationships with influential people who care about you and want you to succeed.

With the tools in this book, Mark will lead you to Camelot, the place where all your dreams and desires will be realized.

You'll live the life you thought you could only dream about. Isn't it time to reward yourself with the gift of learning how to become the ultimate you? Mark will share with you what has helped make him a phenomenal success. As he'll tell you, it can certainly work for you.

Get ready to experience the power in the magic of Mark Victor Hansen as he takes you on the most incredible journey you'll ever undertake—the journey to learn your life's truest passions. Your life will become limitless, and you'll experience it as you never have before. Read on as Mark bridges the ordinary and the extraordinary, showing you how to think bigger than you ever thought you could.

Introduction

The size of your thinking determines the size of your results, your future, and your life. If we can learn to think bigger, live bigger, act bigger, and be bigger, our results are going to be bigger. So will our influence in the world and the universe. How we feel about ourselves will be bigger and better. I want everyone to know how to think big, act big, live big, be big, and get big results.

The benefit of thinking big is enormous. I watched my father go through life saying, "All I want to do is be a good provider for my family." He was, and there's nothing wrong with that, but if I could have instilled in him the ability to think big, instead of having one little bakery and working eighteen hours a day, he could have worked two or three days a week or had a week off every month. He could have had more of a life, more joy with his family, more mind freedom, money freedom, and time freedom than he could even have imagined.

It's all available to you. I'm asking you to go on a little journey through this book. I'll give you some principles, some ideas, techniques, and strategies for thinking bigger and living bigger.

Let me introduce you to some of the world's biggest and best thinkers. Let me be a gadfly that challenges you to be more than you ever thought it could be. In the last chapter, I'm going to talk about realizing Camelot. King Arthur wanted to create that idyllic spot, but each and every one of us can realize our respective Camelots.

Nothing's too good for you. You're entitled to think big. You're entitled to achieve better than your best. I'm cheering you on to a greater, grander, nobler, more important, meaningful, and worthwhile future than you ever expected, so you can leave a legacy that is lasting, purposeful, and memorable.

All of us are born as little thinkers. It's normal and natural.

We come in, and everybody is thinking small, talking small, acting small, and being small. But if you'll go with me through this book, hopefully it will inspire you from the inside out to really become a big thinker. You're going to make your world wonderful, uplifted, exciting, exalted. You're going to take yourself and all the people around you to the Garden of Eden (metaphorically speaking). You're going to have the magic sword Excalibur in your hand, and you're going to be able to conquer things beyond what you currently believe. You're going to get to realize Camelot in your own life. You're to become a King Arthur.

King Arthur is obviously a legend, a metaphor, a myth—something that never was and always is. Big thinking always *is*. If you are made in the image and likeness of God, then we're God stuff and we're good stuff; we're entitled at the depth of our being to think big. When you think big, you achieve big. When you achieve big, you become a beneficial presence in universe. You make a difference. You're worthwhile, your value expands exponentially, everybody is better off, and no one's worse off.

As we learn how to think big together, we're going to make the whole world work for 100 percent of humanity. I'm thankful that you're going to take this little trip with me. I hope it will be the most exhilarating, mind expanding, life enriching trip you've ever been on.

1

Unconscious Competence

Let me start with a story about a friend of mine whom I've known for twenty-five years. Today he's a superstar. He's got an all-time mega best seller called *You Were Born Rich*. He is a speaker that galvanizes your spirit and stabs you awake at levels you didn't know you had.

Bob Proctor's story is a perfect start for learning how to think bigger than you ever thought you could. But it wasn't always that good. Decades ago, Bob was a firefighter in Canada. He was earning the awesome amount of $4,000 a year, and he was $6,000 in debt. Sound familiar?

Bob quit the fire department. His chief and friends thought he was nuts, but he had read a book called *Think and Grow Rich*, by Napoleon Hill. It wowed his soul. He believed its principles. He wrote on an index card that he could earn $25,000 a year. He didn't have a clue how to do it, but he did what the world's greatest self-help action book told him to do and proceeded on faith.

Someone came along and told Bob that he could make great money cleaning offices and windows, so that's where he started. His office cleaning business took off like a rocket. Bob was earning $100 extra a week, then $200 extra, then $300 extra, and suddenly $500 extra, all working by himself. He thought he'd found the keys to the kingdom.

One year later, Bob's business was booming, and he collapsed on the street in Toronto. When he woke up, there was a cop, an ambulance driver, and a very concerned crowd hovering around him. As he sat on the curb, he realized his body was trashed and exhausted. He'd thought the key was to keep working harder to earn his coveted $25,000, but he got the message.

After a few weeks of rest and meditation, Bob had a new plan. From that point on his new motto would be, "If I can't clean them all, I won't clean any of them." He decided to sell and manage the office cleaning business instead.

At the same time, Bob was consistently listening to one of the first inspirational audios ever created: *The Strangest Secret*, by Earl Nightingale. In the tape, Earl says, "Tell me what you want, and I'll tell you how to get it."

Bob decided to sell the cleaning business to employees. He started asking people what they wanted and needed. He sold them what they wanted and showed them how to get it. Bob recruited bank managers and purchasing agents—an unlikely but wonderful smorgasbord of quality people. He did it by finding out what they wanted most.

One banker said, "I want a new car."

Bob said, "I'll give it to you. You give me one hour a night, five nights a week between 5:00 p.m. and 8:00 p.m., and you'll earn $100 extra per month. No one will see you or know except us."

The job got done. The banker got the car. Bob's business grew, and everyone was happy. Bob kept learning and earning. He hired cleaners in Toronto, Montreal, Boston, Atlanta, and London.

By thinking big, he'd conquered an industry and created an empire.

A few years after selling the business, Bob wanted to know why it worked so well. Bob decided to invest his adult life in finding the answer, so he could help others understand and make the process simpler for themselves.

The Rise in Competence

As Bob researched, he discovered he'd been an unconscious competent, a theory first framed by Abraham Maslow, the father of modern self-image psychology. Maslow says we all start out unconsciously *incompetent*.

We don't know we can't tie our shoes, and we don't care. Then a parent says, "Hey, buddy, you can't tie your shoes. Come on; get with it."

Eventually, you become an *unconscious competent*: you know how to tie your shoes and do it really well, without having to think about it. In the highest stages of unconscious competence, our work becomes effortless effort, and we succeed almost in spite of ourselves. Let's see what it means to be an unconscious competent. This is the primary goal of this chapter: teaching you how to become an unconscious competent in big thinking.

Let's quickly review how Bob Proctor worked his way toward unconscious competence. First, it doesn't matter how humble your situation is; there is a solution. Bob had no college education, no connections, and only an idea. Second, Bob badly wanted out of the prison of a low-paying job. Third, he read *Think and Grow Rich*, and that lit his fire. Fourth, he heard of an opportunity and decided the risk was worth the reward. (We only need one blast-off opportunity, and we are launched.) Fifth, during a major setback, he recognized immediately where he'd gone wrong and made immediate changes. Sixth, by listening to his inner thoughts, he had a breakthrough idea that dramatically changed his life: "If I can't do all of the windows, I'm not going to do any of them."

Seventh, Bob sold his cleaning services in several countries for fast expansion. Eighth, he discovered lifelong learning and books and tapes to keep him charging forth. Now, in his eighties, he's not retiring, he's *refiring*. He's going onward, upward, goodward, and Godward.

Finally, Bob believed he could achieve, and did. He became an unconscious competent, and so can you. Throughout these chapter, you'll read examples of ordinary people—some with extreme challenges—living extraordinary lives. You'll be asked to take action and practice certain principles. These exercises are simple and easy, but they must be done regularly for a twenty-one-day period in order to gain some awesome results.

The Power of Twenty-one

That's right. I respectfully ask you to read this book twenty-one times until the ideas become yours. It takes twenty-one days for an old habit or belief to fall to the side and a new one to take its place.

Best-selling author Dr. Maxwell Maltz, a leading plastic surgeon and psychiatrist in the sixties and seventies, discovered this fact. For twenty-one days before their tape was to be removed, he instructed his plastic surgery patients to constantly repeat the phrase, "I'm beautiful, I'm beautiful, I'm beautiful," with feeling and belief. If they didn't follow his instructions, they'd still think of themselves as unattractive, no matter what the world or their friends said. This is called *self-validation*.

Work this twenty-one-day concept, and keep positive, even if you don't see results for the first few days. Make a commitment to follow through for twenty-one days. After all, that's a short time in comparison to your lifetime, and those days will pass whether you make changes for the better or not. Let's make a deal that you'll follow through with this process for a month before you pass judgment.

Imagination and the Dream Team

Next concept: finding dream teamers. I ask you to find another like-minded person who's willing to become a big thinker, too. Someone who will dream-team with you and also read this book twenty-one times in order to make a big difference in their lives. Chapter 8 of this book, entitled "Dream Teaming," explains how to find that perfect person. What's in it for you? A life of majesty, mystery, nobility, and magic. It will be beyond good and it will be beyond beyond.

The next concept is exercising your imagination. Albert Einstein once said, "The significant problems we face cannot be solved at the same level of thinking at which they were created." According to Bob, the solution is to get above the problem to see it from a fresh, clear perspective. He once suggested looking at a problem in terms of a series of lines on a sheet of paper. Say the problem is at line twenty, so metaphorically, let's go up to line ten and look down on the problem from that perspective.

The ideas in this chapter will enable to elevate your thinking so that you can create new solutions, alternatives, and options. You'll find that by creating and working from different ideas, visions, perspectives, and dreams, you'll begin to own them for yourself. You'll be called great, extraordinary, outstanding, impressive, a superstar, a beneficial presence in the world, and a human treasure. All by effectively using the greatest gift, your imagination—and only you can use it.

Of all the creatures in the animal kingdom, God gave imagination to humans alone. Bill Gates said, "The only asset at Microsoft is human imagination." I say, "The only asset any of us has is human imagination." Walt Disney said, "Imagination is the only reality."

Can you believe that in his first job, Walt Disney was told he lacked imagination and ideas? Each of us knows someone who tried to shut us down. You have to be careful not to buy into their ignorance and insufficiency thinking; instead, keep that imagination rolling.

Leverage Big Thinking

Once you've gotten your unconscious competence rolling, created your dream team, and let your imagination loose, the next step is learning how to leverage big thinking.

This concept is based on an economic standard called the three M's. M1 occurs when a person trades his time or her time for money. Unfortunately, that's where 97 percent of Americans live, work, and have their being. M2 is where you invest your money in equities, stocks, bonds, real estate and other assets that pay a healthy return. Your goal is to build up enough wealth and M2 assets that you can comfortably and sustainably live off the income of your assets. It doesn't matter what that figure needs to be: whatever you want and need is available; it can be earned by simply thinking bigger and acting on that big thinking. M3 occurs when you leverage yourself through other people and build a residual ongoing income.

Bob Proctor built up a workforce of hundreds of people doing the work of cleaning offices and office windows. A little residual income earned here and there, multiplied by lots of people, becomes an exponential revenue.

Then there's a secret level beyond these. It's what I call M4 income. This is where you share your ideas for money. In sophisticated terms, it's called selling your intellectual properties: copyrights on books, tapes, videos, special reports, trademarks, licenses, videos, films, franchises, games, pictures, toys, card software, music. You do the work once and get paid for it possibly forever.

Singer-songwriter Paul Anka wrote eight thousand songs. One song, the theme to TV's *The Tonight Show*, was played so often that he could have retired on residuals from that alone.

This is where I live, move, and share my being. I love it. You think once, put it on paper, and either sell it or get others to sell it for you. The world is full of phenomenal distributors, licensees, and sublicensees that can multiply your money virtually overnight. Throughout this book, I'll share thoughts that are designed to trigger your thinking not only as a big thinker but as an exponential thinker.

I'll be sharing stories too. The more we wrap our minds around uplifting, inspirational stories, the bigger and better we will become. We create our new story by hearing a story from someone else that is relevant to our situation.

I guarantee that if you read this entire book, many of these stories will hit you where you live. You will change your perspective, uplift your beliefs, and find solutions to problems you once thought were irresolvable; the ideas will start bubbling. When a great idea surfaces, write it down immediately and record it. If you're driving, pull over and catch your thought flashes. Earl Nightingale said, "Ideas are like wet, slippery fish. You've got to get them when they show up, or they'll slip away, never to be seen again."

Psychologists tell us we have over fifty thousand ideas a day. One great money-making idea is all that it takes. I know you have one sitting right in front of you; cherish it, nurture it, and harvest it. Steven Spielberg made more from product licensing on *E.T. the Extra-Terrestrial* than from the film's breakthrough earnings. L. Frank Baum, an insurance agent, wrote *The Wizard of Oz* for himself and his kids, but it's been made into multiple books and movies, high-school plays, and Halloween costumes that still pay his estate millions every year. Thinking makes it so, so think big. Be open to your own great ideas.

No Time to Lose

The next concept: don't wait to act on your ideas. I tell you earnestly, you have no time to lose. You are gifted with natural, automatic ability to achieve your goals, but every day I meet people who are just sitting there, waiting for their ship to come in. They will wait for a lifetime, because they haven't sent a ship out yet. Stop waiting. It's time to realize the great gifts you can offer the world. If you let your gifts go unnoticed, unused, and unannounced, they'll be wasted and cannot be reclaimed later.

The first actions you take to fulfill your dreams will probably be less than perfect. There's no such thing as a flawless attempt towards success, but you can't let that stop you from moving forward now. Standup comedians Robin Williams, Steve Martin, Steven Wright, and Whoopi Goldberg had many nights in front of stone-faced crowds. I'm sure before chefs like Wolfgang Puck or Julia Child created mouthwatering masterpieces, they set a kitchen or two on fire. Before entrepreneurs like Ted Turner, W. Clement Stone, or Mary Kay Ash became multimillionaires, they suffered an assortment of rejections, disappointments, bankruptcies, and setbacks. No matter what your goal is, it will never be accomplished perfectly. You must start right now where you are, with what you have. *Think and Grow Rich* says, "Begin at once, whether you're ready or not."

Become aware of what's possible. Awareness is like a twenty-four-story skyscraper. Every one of us is born at the bottom, naked, helpless, and ignorant. Everyone is somewhere in that building, going up or down. The top floor is called *total God awareness.*

Some people aren't even aware there's an elevator in this building. Let this book open your eyes and point you to your own elevator. Now get in and move on up. Once you move toward your dreams, you stop worrying. You're aware of the opportunity and time to take advantage of them. You can avert danger before it occurs.

When I was a student traveling with the visionary thinker Dr. R. Buckminster Fuller, we got on a plane and he quietly told me, "Grab everything and get off now." That plane crashed. It killed everyone on board.

Fuller was enlightened at a high level. I'd say he was somewhere near the top of this metaphorical skyscraper.

At the time, I couldn't see what he saw, but now I've learned to see it.

Find a Mentor

The next powerful concept is studying with mentors. By studying people on the floors above you, you learn to see their levels faster. My colleague Dr. Wayne Dyer wrote a book called *Wisdom of the Ages: Sixty Days to Enlightenment,* about sixty leaders, thinkers, and self-actualized people he had devoted his life to studying. These thoughtful biographical studies will definitely expand your thinking and give you a more eclectic point of view. Such books inspire us to believe that we too can move from ordinary to extraordinary.

I'd like you to do an exercise. Ask everyone you meet who they think the biggest thinker in the world is or was. Take copious notes, or record your sessions. I predict you'll have the most extraordinary conversations of your life; you'll discover what people are really thinking or not thinking. You'll learn things that will delight, excite, wow, and even stun you. You'll have entered into a real university of life. Suddenly you're on an accelerated learning curve on which every great thinker, leader, and self-realized person has traveled. Watch where they go; follow their path.

I have great admiration for one of the greatest speakers of our time, Cavett Robert. Cavett was a dean of

American speakers and the cofounder of the National Speakers Association. Cavett was also the creator of self-help audios and offered a platform to help audience members get into personal growth and development.

At age sixty-two, Cavett was speaking on a topic: are you the cause or are you the result? Sony had just created its first generation of Walkman tape recorders. Until that night, people who wanted to avail themselves of audio learning methods had to listen to record albums in their living rooms, because the information wasn't portable.

Cavett, speaking to seven thousand Rotarians, announced for the first time ever that he had a tape of his session available with a Sony Walkman. To Cavett's amazement, every one of the seven thousand attendees invested in the tape that Cavett had recorded, along with this new portable gadget.

Cavett was so surprised that, he told me, it kept him awake for three nights, wondering how he could repeat what he had said to help others. Little did he know that he just launched an industry that would only three decades later be selling billions of dollars' worth of educational audio materials. Thousands of speakers, teachers, and trainers across the planet have benefited from Cavett's experiment.

Who are your mentors? Can you find examples of big thinking in today's modern culture? How about Oprah Winfrey? Oprah was born in the Deep South and was pregnant by the time she was fourteen. She says she was born with no voice, no influence, no power, and no money. She was abused, tormented, and beaten, but through it all, she learned how to read and write. In her journal, she wrote that one day she would be on the cover of *Vanity Fair* magazine and *TV Guide*. It seemed almost impossible, because she saw herself as fat, frumpy, and dumpy.

Then Oprah met Bob Greene, an exercise coach who convinced her that she could transform her image, energy, and life by exercising twice a day. Exercising not only transformed her life but her future. She represents what is truly achievable.

We can all inwardly say, "If Oprah can do it, I can do it." It's not just a matter of *can*, it's a matter of *will*. Tell yourself this: "If she did it, I will do it." If you have the discipline to get it done, you can set your life on fire.

Where can you begin? Right now. Build something every day to realize a life-transforming dream.

Ray's Triumph

Ray Kroc never thought he'd be in the hamburger business. He thought he was doing well enough with his new milkshake machine, called the Multimixer. Brothers Mac and Dick McDonald bought eight all at once. Surprised at the large order, Ray Kroc went to San Bernardino, California, to see what the McDonald brothers were doing that would require eight multimixers for one location.

When Ray arrived, he couldn't believe his eyes. From 11:00 a.m. in the morning till 2:30 p.m., the drive-in parking lot was packed with customers. The McDonalds ran a clean operation, with a simple menu, offering hamburgers for 15 cents, French fries, milkshakes, soft drinks, and coffee.

That night, Ray had visions of McDonald drive-ins dotting the American countryside, eight of his Multimixers residing in each one. The next day he asked the brothers if they'd ever considered expansion. "Everything is peaceful," they told him, "With expansion comes problems. We just want to enjoy what we have. See that big house up on hill? That's ours, and we're comfortable in it."

Ray suggested that they could find someone else to open all the restaurants for them.

"Who?" asked Dick.

Before he realized he was saying it, Ray asked, "How about me?"

The McDonald brothers signed expansion rights to Ray that very day. In 1954, few people were familiar with the concept of a drive-in restaurant, let alone the concept of franchising. Ray was fifty-four years old, he had diabetes, arthritis, and a nonfunctioning gallbladder, but he was convinced the best was ahead of him. Ray's first outlet was in Des Plaines, Illinois, in 1955. When he lacked money for expansion, he went to Coca-Cola, his supplier, and shared his story. They liked it. They extended his terms of payments to help him grow. Today McDonald's is the biggest seller of Coca-Cola in the world. As of 2018, McDonald's was serving 60 million customers in nearly 38,000 restaurants worldwide.

Find Hidden Opportunities

The next concept: look for hidden and overlooked opportunities. This is more of a *wow* than an idea. Often we see more potential in someone else's opportunity than they can. Keep your eyes open for underused resources, assets, talents, products and services. They exist everywhere. Your opportunity is to see them and capitalize on them.

Peter John de Savary was refused ownership in his father's furniture business. Rather than wallow in that disappointment, he sold his house and car, moved his family to Holland, and began looking for a new opportunity.

Shortly thereafter, he was offered an import-export business for £3,000, then equivalent to about $6,000. He wrote a business plan to raise £6,000—half to buy the business and the remaining half to buy tropical suits, an impressive briefcase, and a first-class ticket to Africa. Everyone except one young lawyer thought it would be a bad investment.

On his first flight, Peter sat in first class on a plane to Nigeria next to Moses Gowon, a retiring Nigerian Air Force pilot en route to becoming a civilian. Nigeria at the time was a country of 62 million people just beginning to rebuild after a civil war; both men were business novices and decided to work together. They sealed the deal with a handshake. The next day Gowon called Peter, telling him there was a particular official he wanted him to meet. On the way to the appointment, Peter asked, "Who is this guy?"

To which Gowon replied, "He's my brother. The president of Nigeria."

The rest is history. Peter stood in front of the most powerful man in Nigeria, whose country needed everything but the rich oil they produced. They commissioned Peter to go back to Europe and bring all the products and services—food, agriculture—he could think of. Peter's income and influence soared. He bought and renovated Andrew Carnegie's beloved Skibo Castle in Scotland, along with the eight thousand-acre playground that accompanied it.

Need, Greed, and Freed

How can you do what these people have done? Let's talk about three words that at first might seem a little abrasive, but let's discuss them and see if you don't agree: *need*, *greed*, and *freed*. It's simple. First, teach yourself to see the *need* and the *greed* in order to act on opportunities that will lead you to being *freed.* Evolution of growth always goes through these three stages.

We all start out in need. We're born naked, helpless, ignorant, independent. My wife and I used to hide our giggles when our baby daughter Melanie would whine, "Help me. Somebody, please help me," while she was sitting in a sink naked, getting a bath. She grew out of it, but some people remain locked in their need phase. They don't want to show up, grow up, and live up to their God-given potential.

For those of us who do go on, we hit the greed phase. You can be greedy for love, friendship, fame, money, or whatever. It comes from the belief that there's not enough to go around and that you yourself are not enough. In 1798, British economist Thomas Malthus predicted that India would eat itself out of existence. He didn't understand that with right thinking, we can create more than enough so that no one needs to be greedy. That's freedom.

Malthus couldn't imagine refrigeration, transportation, irrigation, hybridization, crop rotation, intercropping, or hydroponics. Today these things are part of our lives. You can bear witness to all the wonders of the freed stage by visiting Epcot Center at Disney World. The craft exhibit alone shows how we can feed everyone alive right here and now and continue to do so sustainably into the future.

"I'm Enough"

Let's talk about positive affirmations. As I've just mentioned, the second reason for greed is the "I'm not enough" syndrome. Occasionally, we all feel that we're not enough, so we must continually work on building ourselves up to overcome feelings of inadequacy. We must constantly and continuously affirm ourselves positively. Affirmations are the words that you say to yourself: you believe, think about, act upon them, and then that they act upon you.

I'd like to give you an assignment of saying fifty times a day, "I'm enough. I'm enough. I'm enough. I'm enough. I'm enough." You can do different voice intonations, but say this sentence fifty times a day until it goes deep into your subconscious. At first utter it quietly and in private, then stand in front of a mirror and say it, then say it in your car and as you head into meetings. It's amazing. It's transformational. As you go up in an elevator, just quietly rehearse, "I'm enough. I'm enough. I'm enough. I'm enough." You'll come out with inner strength and a new self-image, along with a new realization of what you can do.

Faith without Fear

Next concept: practice faith without fear. I know sometimes fear and obstacles get in your way. In the Bible, God saved Daniel from the jaws of the lions. Daniel wanted to practice his faith in God, and the king wasn't at all pleased with his spiritual petitions. The king sent Daniel to the lion's den with a parting comment, "Your God, whom you serve continually, will deliver you."

Early the next morning, the king rose and went to the lion's den, and there was Daniel waving at him in perfect health. He said, "My God sent his angel and shut the lion's mouth, so they have not hurt me."

Daniel's absolute faith allowed him to face the lions fearlessly. Not smelling fear on this man, the lions merely thought him an interesting addition to the den.

When you're cast into the lion's den, so to speak, stay conscious, stay in tune with the infinite good and the infinite God, and you'll remain unscathed. If you let fear and intimidation take you away, you'll be eaten alive. Take control of your life, your destiny, your path; play it the way you want to play it, and even the rulers and the rule makers of the world will see that you are free.

Take Control of Your Life

Next application: take control of your life and your future. Don't hesitate to audit or taste-test all the courses you want whether in school or with self-advancement books, audios, and videos. Remember, you deserve the very best.

Today, thanks to the Internet, you have it available to you. Use the same auditing theory that I used with my child's education. My children attend public school. Before my first daughter, Elizabeth, began school, I physically sat in six kindergarten classes. The last class I experienced was with Mrs. Cathy Fellows. She was great. She had it together, and her results were clicking. The kids loved her. She talked and taught both in English and Spanish. She had them stand and create each letter of the alphabet with their bodies, saying, "I'm an X"; "I'm a Y"; "I'm a T." Then she had each kid roll up into a shape of a doughnut and say, "I'm a Q," while sticking out their tongues. It's called kinesthetic learning.

Because I sat in that class, both Elizabeth and her little sister, Melanie, enjoyed life and learning greatly from Mrs. Fellows. We also invited each teacher over to our house for dinner with our kids before school began. They left our house knowing that we wanted excellence out of our kids and excellence out of them. The teachers had the freedom to call us if anything wasn't going according to plan.

I want to support and improve the public-school system. In order to do so, I want to participate. I want you to do so, too. As you take an active, hands-on interest in your kids' education, their grades and attitudes improve. Teachers feel comfortable with a shared partnership of educating your child. Everyone wins.

Now that's big thinking. Too often we allow ourselves to be intimidated away from our own power. Don't. If you want to know what your future outcomes will be, create them.

It's All in Your Head

The next application that I think is relevant is, it's all in your head. Big thinking ultimately provides security for you and your family's future, because you and I are secured from the inside out, not from the outside in. You can have the world's treasures and still be paranoid that they'll be gone tomorrow, or you can have the ultimate security, which is an inside job, and know that you could replace it all if you had to, because your mind created it all in the first place.

Paul J. Meyer, a business giant, philanthropist, and author of *I Inherited a Fortune*, eloquently stated, "Whatever you can vividly imagine, ardently desire, sincerely believe, and enthusiastically act upon must inevitably come to pass." Paul was a business tycoon, the owner of eighty-three active companies. He was a self-made millionaire at twenty-one. That's way past greed and totally into being freed. Steve Wynn decided he'd recreate Las Vegas by creating the Bellagio casino—an exemplification of quality, romance and elegance.

Dream big, live big, act big, think big, and big results will be yours. Then you're going to be unstoppable, and you'll be free. When you have set your mind free, the physical world can't constrain you.

Remember, a company or business is just the body of the car; your mind is the engine. It's not what you've acquired, but who you are that determines your wealth. The challenge is to live up to the opportunity. The Golden Age is here. It's now. You're a vital part of it. Your eighty-six billion brain cells will tune in, turn on, and make it so. You can blast off to big thinking. If you're feeling a little tentative, I'll cover that in the next chapter, "Converting Your Fear into Rocket Fuel."

I hope to ignite your rocket ship and to find you eager, ready, and waiting to blast off to success beyond your wildest dreams and greatest aspirations.

Move toward greatness by starting with yourself. Each of us is the CEO and president of our own lives. We need to personally take responsibility for where we've been, where we are, and where we are going.

The following words were written on the tomb of an Anglican bishop in the crypts of London's Westminster Abbey.

When I was young and free, my imagination had no limits. I dreamed of changing the world. As I grew older and wiser, I discovered the world would not change. I shortened my sights somewhat and decided to change my country, but it too seemed immovable. As I grew into my twilight years, in one last desperate attempt, I settled for changing only my family, those closest to me, but alas, they would have none of it. Now, as I lie on my deathbed, I suddenly realize that if only I changed myself first, then by example, I would have changed my family. From their inspiration and encouragement, I then would be able to better my country, and who knows? I may have even changed my world.

2

Converting Your Fear
into Rocket Fuel

If you've ever had a challenge in life, a real problem, a setback, or a letdown, you know the pain that comes from being unable to bypass it. You also know that the more quickly you can address and resolve problems, the more quickly you can move on with your life.

In this chapter, I'll show you how to remove the pain from your life in as little as twenty-one days by thinking your way past your problems and fears.

Fear is faith in a wrong thing. Fear is embracing and believing in a negative image and negative outcome. Unfortunately, all of us get sucked into fear, but now we're going to convert it into rocket fuel.

"If I Had Only Known"

To begin with, everyone has fear. The good news is that we can convert our fears into rocket fuel, and I'm going to teach you how.

Let me share a fear handling story with you that offers several applications. Jana Stanfield writes songs that are in *Chicken Soup for the Soul*. I'm going to share with you her most famous lyrics, from a song sung by country artist Reba McEntire. Reba took this song to triple platinum in remembrance of members of her band who were killed in a plane crash.

If I had only known
It was our last walk in the rain
I'd keep you out for hours in the storm
I would hold your hand
Like a lifeline to my heart
Underneath the thunder we'd be warm
If I had only known
It was our last walk in the rain

If I had only known
I'd never hear your voice again
I'd memorize each thing you ever said
And on these lonely nights,
I could think of them once more

And keep your words alive inside my head
If I had only known
I'd never hear your voice again

You were the treasure in my heart
You were the one who always stood beside me
So unaware, I foolishly believed
That you would always be there
But then there came a day when I closed my eyes
And you slipped away

If I had only known
It was my last night by your side
I'd pray a miracle would stop the dawn
And when you smiled at me,
I would look into your eyes
And make sure you know my love for you goes on and on
If I had only known,
If I had only known
The love I would've shown
If I had only known

Jana told me that the song might never have been created if she'd received her driver's license the same day as her friends did. Her story goes like this. "In Clovis, New Mexico, where I was raised, you get your driver's license at age fifteen. Nearly everybody in my class turned fifteen during the ninth grade. On the last day of school, if they passed their driver's ed test, they could get their licenses.

"Even though I wouldn't turn fifteen until I started the tenth grade, I was thrilled that my friends would be driving. The excitement and anticipation on that final day of junior high was almost unbearable to us. Never again would we have to be hauled around like cattle by our mothers. At last, we would be free.

"My dad saw the situation differently. He didn't think my friends would be safe drivers yet. He was afraid I would wind up in an accident and didn't want me to go places with them until we started school again in the fall. So I worked for my Aunt Dorothy at a car place that summer. I was in my awkward teenage years, and she was really good to me. By the end of that summer, I'd saved enough money to buy all my own clothes for school. I started high school feeling different in a good way—older, stronger, and more confident.

"After that summer, I didn't have much time to see my Aunt Dorothy. When I graduated from college, she gave me a beautiful bracelet, and underneath the cotton was a gift even more precious to me. Folded up small was a dusty old sheet of stationery that said, 'My name is Jana Lee Stanfield, stars shining bright above me. Never will I have chicken feet for breakfast.'

"Six years later, I was living in Nashville, trying without much success to be a songwriter, when Aunt Dorothy was diagnosed with cancer. Not long after, I got a call that Aunt Dorothy was slipping away quickly but was still well enough to talk on the phone if I wanted to say good-bye. Holding the slip of paper with the phone number, I thought about how the smallest thing a person does with love can make the biggest difference in our lives.

"Calling Aunt Dorothy that day was one of the most painful things I've ever experienced," said Jana. "I told her how much I loved her. I thanked her for reaching out to me when I needed somebody.

"I didn't want to hang up. I wanted to stop the clock and go back and spend more time with her. After Aunt Dorothy and I said our last 'I love you,' I hung up the phone and sobbed into the silence of an empty apartment. I thought about all of the people who touch our lives with their kindness and then disappear before we ever thank them. On a lonely Sunday a few weeks later, the words, 'If Only I Had Known' came in a flood of tears.

"Since I didn't know much about writing melodies yet, I took the unfinished lyrics to the most talented song-writer I knew, Craig Morris, and asked if he would craft something beautiful. In the same way that Aunt Dorothy turned my life around when I was fourteen, she had turned it around again by inspiring 'If Only I Had Known.'"

Jana touches my heart. Her pain touches everyone's heart, because she speaks to every person's life, adventures, and struggles. She gives us strength, hope, help, and encouraging words that can be rocket fuel to blast past our fears. She understood that you have to dream bigger than your fears.

After college in Albuquerque, Jana was a TV news anchor, chasing ambulances and taking up someone else's dream job. During that time, she survived a nearly fatal car crash that stopped her in her tracks and forced her to rethink her life's purpose and passion. She decided she wanted to write, sing, and perform in Nashville. She packed up her car and moved from Albuquerque to Nashville, listening to motivational speakers the whole way there.

Jana was convinced she would meet the decision makers at the big Nashville record companies, get bookings, and get a contract. Instead, she was put on hold with a heart full of disappointment. Rather than waiting for her ship to come in, she acted. She started her own company, which guaranteed that whatever she wrote would get published. As Jana told me, a dream is a direction, not a destination. It guides us to have the courage to follow our dreams. It will teach us what we need to know.

How can Jana's story apply to your life? First, don't compromise your dream job or hold space in someone else's dream job. Second, she made her dream greater, bigger, stronger than her fear. When your dream takes on size and strength, obstacles tend to melt away. Third, it's OK to be disappointed. When your dream is on hold, don't get discouraged. Discouragement stops you in your tracks. Fourth, no matter how many setbacks and upsets, decide you're going to blast through them anyway. Fifth, if you're off purpose or doing what you shouldn't be doing, God gives you a gentle and progressively stronger warning signal. Jana's was a car accident; mine was bankruptcy. To prevent such an awful experience, get meditative and reflective. Have your journal ready, and ask, "What is my right livelihood?"

Sixth, pay attention. Listen to your inner ear. If the red light on your car dashboard comes on, you pay attention. Look for those red lights in your life. Seventh, understand that you may not be accepted or even welcomed. Jana got to Nashville and was not welcomed with the kind of love, expectancy, and joy she was hoping for, but she handled it. You can handle it, too. Remember, it's not about personal rejection, so get out there again and get creative.

When no recording company wanted her, Jana started her own recording company. The point here is there's always a way. There's always an innovative alternative to your goal, dream, or heartfelt destination. Make it happen.

Clarity Is Power

The second concept I want to cover here is, clarity is power. When you are clear, you conquer your fears. Most obstacles are more in our minds than in our actual experience.

Imagine that there's a rocket in your life. Sometimes we will feel we're outside the rocket and we're holding on for dear life. The goal, of course, is to get inside the rocket and be comfortable, in total control of your thinking and your feelings. Know in your soul that your story is your life. As your read other people's stories in this book, find your story in theirs. It'll change the way you ride your life and take control of its direction.

Don't let fear of the unknown stand in your way. Learn to study the fear and the challenges, and then change your perception of them. When TV was invented, movie producers feared that it would kill their business. Instead, it exposed movies in a favorable way and multiplied movie viewership. When VCRs became popular in the seventies, again movie producers feared the worst, and again it funded the largest expansion ever in moviemaking—so large, in fact, that Michael Eisner, head of Disney, went from making five feature films a year to fifty-five films a year.

When fear steps in your path, take a good, clean look at it, and you'll find it's just a figment of your imagination. When I worked as a research assistant for Dr. Buckminster Fuller, he wanted all of us to maximize our growth experiences by learning to fly an airplane. Bucky, as he was affectionately called, wanted us to feel the wings of the plane, feel our depth perception and the area encompassed by the plane, and know the feeling of soaring.

After eight hours of training, I was ready for my solo flight. There I was, up in the air, alone at about three thousand feet. My instructor said to stall the plane. At first, out of fear, I held the controls, which would guarantee that I would plummet into the earth. The plane started spinning down uncontrollably. In a nanosecond, a statement in the pilot's instruction manual flashed through my mind: "In a stall, release the controls, and the plane will automatically go into straight, level flight."

I'd just descended fifteen hundred feet and was still going in the wrong direction at an accelerating rate. I released the controls. Blood was gushing into my head. Adrenaline was pumping. I could feel my heart working its way right out of my chest. The plane went into straight, level flight. My instructor said, "Congratulations, big guy. I thought you and the end were going to become one."

After that, I became a much better student. I learned to appreciate the flight simulator. Every six months, every commercial pilot is tested, trained, and retrained on a flight simulator. They drill, practice, and rehearse for zero-defect flying. If they fail and crash the flight simulator, they're instantly fired.

I've watched pilots walk out of a flight simulator rooms blanched white, with sweat dripping underneath their arms down to the back of their legs, with perspiration squishing in their shoes. They know they have to faultlessly execute the right procedures in the right way every time in order to get the right result, right here and now. You've got to rehearse so that in emergencies, you need only rely on your correctly instilled habits to get the right results. When you hit those obstacles, you'll find yourself blasting through them.

Don't be stopped. Statesman Elihu Root once said, "Men don't fail; they give up trying." Usually it's stopping at the wrong time rather than starting at the wrong time that causes failure. In *Think and Grow Rich*, Napoleon Hill tells the story of a prospector who gave up digging for gold. The next prospector picked up where he left off and three feet beyond found one of the biggest strikes of all time.

Look back at the times in your life when you were excited about an idea but hit an obstacle and lost your enthusiasm. You may have been walking away from a gold mine.

When you're building the momentum to achieve your life dreams, you have to keep the flames of desire burning deep inside your heart, no matter what. See your desired end result fulfilled, feel as though it has been accomplished, and you'll accomplish it.

Get Help

Practical application number two: get uplifting help into your life. When I was going bankrupt, I was immobilized with fear. The law of polarity says, "You're either immobilized and stopped, stifled, and thwarted, or you're mobilized, and you're taking vital, life fulfilling action."

I was afraid of every phone call; I was afraid that it'd be a haranguing bill collector. My spiritual, mental, and physical system shut down. I wanted to escape into sleep and never wake up again. Miraculously—and it really was a miracle—I chose to listen to Cavett Robert's tape as I lay in bed.

Cavett's energy wowed my soul, perked me up, and reignited my exhausted system. He stimulated new ideas and new life energy. I listened and relistened to that one tape 287 times, and I got the message. Suddenly, I was mobilized, energized, and activized. Since then, I've helped millions of others do the same or better. I want everyone to fulfill their destiny, live their impossible dream, and go beyond their best.

I've become a positively addicted audio listener. I've listened to over ten thousand hours' worth of audio material. There's so much input that I have ideas spilling out of me, and you will too. These audios keep converting my fears into rocket fuel.

Each of us is occasionally alone and perhaps lonely. Listening to uplifting speakers rejuvenates your spirit and helps you realize that you can conquer your world and your life again.

To be exceptional, you have to have consistently exceptional input. Just as you need daily vitamins for your body, you need daily input for your soul.

Think for Yourself

Decades ago (long before the coronavirus led to actual shortages), TV talk show host Johnny Carson announced a run on toilet paper. People believed this joke and actually created a run on toilet paper. One day, it disappeared off the market shelves; people hoarded it and filled their garages with it.

Come on now: start thinking for yourself. Keep your own counsel, and refuse to be poisoned by groupthink and negative propagandizing media.

Fears keep people from their full potential and in time turns into obsessing. You, however, possess the power to overcome your fears and make them disappear. The law of polarity teaches that life is a balance: duality, black and white, concave and convex, in and out, entropy and syntropy. If fear immobilizes us, the polar opposite—action—mobilizes us. Take action, and fear disappears.

We're entitled to greater good because we can conceive greater good. Fear and suffering can never be imposed upon us unless we impose it on ourselves. The same goes for joy. The spirit can give us no gift that we do not give ourselves permission to accept.

Your belief system sets the expanse or limits of what you can receive. Because Principle is infinite, you can have as much or as little as you conceive.

Belief systems are interesting. Each of us has one that can shape, shift, and morph. Before 1954, every runner believed that if you ran under a four-minute mile, your heart would jump out of your chest. Roger Bannister, a British medical doctor, didn't believe it. That year he was the first person ever to run a mile in 3:59 minutes. The world cheered, applauded, and celebrated his breakthrough. Here's the interesting fact: within one month, his record was broken. Within one year, nineteen people ran a mile in under four minutes. Dr. Bannister's great accomplishments can inspire each of us to attempt something great, because it can go on to change the world's perspective.

When you clearly and definitely know what you want and are dedicated to getting it, you will. Each of us has to get definite with the infinite. In my case, I want to be the first self-help action author to sell one billion books by 2030. I call it my perfect 2030 vision.

As I put this thought out, I want you to explain to me how it can be done, because I haven't figured it out yet.

When it comes to talking about your goals, there are two theories you can follow. Either tell no one your goals—that way, no one can call you on them—or tell everyone your goals. They will either cheer for you or ridicule you. Don't let that fear cripple, crush, or limit you. Let people know where you stand, where you want to stand, and push the edge of your envelope in the world's envelope. You'll be amazed at the response and support you'll ultimately receive.

The Danish philosopher Søren Kierkegaard said, "Great dreamers' dreams are never fulfilled. They're always transcended." I want you to have great goals, then transcend them. When you share your idea with like-minded, highly motivated, energized people, miracles happen. The size of your dream, added to an unbeatable team, will deliver your scheme.

What four-minute mile are you going to break so that everyone else can break it too? You have one issue, one problem, one dream, one great and inspiring possibility that is yours and yours alone. Only you can do it for all of us.

You have a life assignment. I believe it was coded in you at DNA and RNA level, and as you reflect upon yourself, you'll find it. We have a charity attached to each of our books, such The Chicken Soup for the Soul Cookbook. We invented the chicken soup concept and subsequently turned it into a cookbook. How are we going to help the masses with it? In other words, what is our ripple effect going to be?

One Thanksgiving, we were working with Warren Curry, who was running the Union Rescue Mission on LA's Skid Row. Warren's energy is pure, sincere, loving, helpful, and quietly effective. I see him as a Mother Teresa type in a male body. He was feeding four thousand people a day and sleeping a thousand people a night.

Warren met a young woman out on the streets. As Warren talked to her, he realized she was well educated and well spoken. He discovered that she was from Grosse Pointe, Michigan—an affluent community. She had an affair and was so ashamed that she left her family and ran away to LA, where she became homeless. He helped her to overcome her fears, got her cleaned up, and called her family for her. She forgave herself, her relatives forgave her, and better yet, they responded immediately. They showed up to take her home right in the middle of our Turkey Day event, when we were feeding ten thousand people. They all cheered and celebrated with her and her family. Think of the ripple effect that that one action caused.

Don't Let the Odds Take You Down

I firmly believe that no obstacle is too great to force to you to give up your dream.

When Og Mandino was five years old, his mother told him that he'd be a great writer. He came back from World War II and tried selling his writing talent, but had absolutely no success. Things got worse. His family and business evaporated from underneath him. In his opinion, he became a useless alcoholic. He wanted to end it all but didn't even have the courage to buy a gun.

Chilled to the bone in the cold New Hampshire winter, Og went into the library for warmth. He sat at a table feeling rejected, dejected, and hopeless. A book practically fell in front of him called *A Success System That Never Fails* by W. Clement Stone, one of the world's richest and most philanthropic men. He read it, believed it, and decided he wanted to work for Mr. Stone. He walked to Chicago, got hired and trained, and proved hugely successful as a salesman. Eventually, Og was promoted to editor of *Success Magazine*. While there, he would occasionally write a short article for the magazine.

As it turns out, the owner of Frederick Fell Publishers was sitting in his dentist's waiting room. He randomly picked up a copy of *Success Magazine*, read one of Og's articles, and loved it. He contacted Og and asked if he'd ever considered writing a book. That's how Og wrote the multimillion best seller *The Greatest Salesman in the World*.

See how actions in the right direction ultimately reap big rewards. It's a ripple effect that, granted, may take a while to gain. But once it gets going, it never stops.

Burn the Fuel on the Front End

Do you need to sacrifice first to make it big? The answer is a big yes. Something or someone out there wants you to prove your determination. You've got to give before you get, and you've got to give big-time, but believe me, it'll pay off big-time.

Motivational speaker Jim Rohn has jokingly told me that no one can beat you if you don't sleep. Now you may not have to work that hard, but then again, you may. At some level, you've got to get out of balance to get back into balance.

It takes 60 percent of all the fuel on board just to lift a plane off the runway. Once you get into your flight pattern, you pull back, and it's cruise time. Your life follows a very same principle. You've got to burn it on the front end to reach cruising altitude. You've got to work really hard and really long at the front, so at the back end you can work a little and get a whole lot.

Sometimes you have to go so deep and sacrifice so much that it opens up a level of consciousness and expands talents and resources you didn't even know you had. What a ride it'll turn out to be!

Again, I want you to understand that everyone occasionally experiences fear. Recognize it for what it is, and work to quickly, safely, and satisfyingly convert it into rocket fuel. All it takes is right thinking, right talking, right acting, and doing the right thing to get the right results, right here and right now. Right thinking vanishes fear, right talking beats it out of existence, and right action makes it disappear.

3

Dare to Dream

My partner Jack Canfield, the dean of self-esteem, teaches what he calls the poker chip theory of life. It is simply this: in the game of life, if you have ten poker chips and I have a hundred, who's going to bet more heavily and feel more comfortable betting? Obviously, the person with a hundred poker chips has more to play with and less to lose. Therefore whoever has the most poker chips can bet the biggest and potentially win the most.

The poker chips for you in your life are your self-esteem, the size of your thinking, and your belief in your ability to realize your dreams. You're in control. Your self-esteem and subsequent successes are entirely based on how much work you do in and on yourself to make yourself a masterpiece.

Let me go one step further. In the movie *Jerry Maguire*, Cuba Gooding Jr. plays a football star who says to his agent, Jerry, "Show me the money." That's how every little thinker thinks: "When I see it, I'll believe it." Big thinkers, on the other hand, say, "When I believe it, I'll see it." The real poker chips in life are your belief system. What you think and believe, you can achieve.

Write Out 101 Goals

Let me start this chapter with the Mark Victor Hansen challenge: I want you to write out 101 goals in twenty minutes. If you don't have any goals, then your goal is to set some goals and set them now. The psychologist Erik Erikson said, "Give yourself a thought command, such as, 'I can write my goals in twenty minutes today,' and your subconscious will figure out how to get that job done."

Act as if your life or more importantly, the life of one of your children depends on your doing this assignment, because in fact it does: goal setting is goal getting.

This process can sound intimidating, but don't let that stop you. Have fun with it. Pretend you're twelve years old. Back then, you were self-reliant, imaginative, and invincible. Every twelve-year-old thinks he or she can do anything and everything.

My twelve-year-old daughter's first goal was an Arabian horse. She earned her own Arabian horse, and his name was Star Man. How did she do it?

We have an organic plum tree, and one night, after she had written down her goal, I came home from work. She had a giant sign in the front yard, which said, "Very affordable plums: $1 a bag."

I said, "Lizzie, how's business?" She said, "Daddy, I'm earning $42 an hour." Now she wouldn't have done that if she didn't have a goal. Isn't it nice to be naive and ignorant about what reality looks like?

As you're writing your goals, don't judge them or go back and read them. You'll have plenty of time for critiquing later. Just write down every idea that comes into your mind—big, small, material, immaterial, tangible, intangible. Include goals about the kind of person you want to be, the talent you want to discover, and how you want to grow within yourself. I can guarantee that no matter what you dream up, God has already provided you with the tools to achieve it. But to achieve it, you've got to believe it first.

I want you to put this book down right here and now. Get out a pad of paper, pull out your computer or your journal, start writing, and don't come back to me until you've got 101 goals in your list. Remember, you're going to do it in twenty minutes; you're going to pretend you're twelve years old.

Here's a bonus idea. I want you to rub your hands vigorously for about a minute. Then pull them about an inch and a half apart, feel that great, pulsating energy, then expand it. Pretend you have a Halloween body mask in front of you, and imbue it with wisdom. Then take that over your head and drape it down to your feet.

I want you to come from wisdom. If it's good enough for Solomon, it's good enough for you. Have wisdom as one of your 101 goals.

Remember, you're not writing your goals in marble. You can erase them, cross them out, redo them. When you achieve each of your goals, I want you to write "Victory" next to it in purple. That's the highest, most spiritual color in the electromagnetic spectrum.

Prioritize Your Goals

Now that you've written down your 101 goals, I want you to prioritize them and write dates next to them. Remember, a goal is a dreamy notion with a deadline. If you're saying, "What if it doesn't work?" I might come right back to you and say, "What if it does?" You're already up to 101 goals. You've already got new results, new relationships, new bragging rights coming together for you, right now even as you hit. Figure out just when you want these dreams to hit, and that's going to be the most enjoyable part of all.

Here's an easy tool to help you with your priorities. First, go through your list quickly, and mark them as A's, B's, and C's. Then divide them again: A1, A2, B1, B2, C1, C2, C3.

Then draw one of those tournament grids that you've seen whenever several teams are competing for a big trophy, like in tennis. Everyone starts on the left side, and game by game the teams are matched up until one emerges victorious.

Match your goals against one another until you have two that pull in front of all the others. Let's say the final two goals having a new home and earning $400,000 yearly. If you're earning $400,000 yearly, you can easily afford your dream home, so the money wins in that berth.

Send me a copy of your goals, and I'll send them back to you one year later. You'll be astonished to discover how ten of them virtually accomplished themselves in the first week, and 60–70 percent of them in the first year.

The Learning Revolution, a book by Gordon Dryden and Jeannette Vos, compiles many of the greatest accelerated-learning methods. One way to learn fast is to have music as your backdrop. If you're creating a calm atmosphere, the authors suggest relaxing music like *Watermark* by Enya. However, if you're setting goals, play *Chariots of Fire* by Vangelis. If you're just doing visualizations, listen to Pachelbel's *Canon in D*, although these authors recommend *Waterfalls* by Paul Lloyd Warner, Michael Jones' *Sunset*, or George Winston's *December*. Jeannette Vos has also done audios on how to accelerate your learning with music. She says because music can both calm and stimulate, it offers one of the quickest ways to influence mood.

Why not use it in your learning? Why not use it in your life beyond romance? Why not use it at the dinner table? Why not use it everywhere?

Map Out Your Plan

Now I want you to map out your plan. A goal, as I said, is simply a dreamy destination with a deadline. After setting goals, your mind will automatically start achieving them by mapping them out. The subconscious figures out how to do that, so don't worry about it.

Here's how Jack Canfield and I mapped out our plan for *Chicken Soup for the Soul*. It ultimately became a whole business plan, but here's where it started. We wrote 1,094 yellow stickies with our ideas on how to sell a million and a half copies in a year and a half. We stuck them on the wall in front of our faces; as I said, we prioritized them. A year and a half later, we'd sold 1.3 million copies. However, without a definite, positive, and specific goal, we never would have done it. Goals have to be in writing, and they have to be measurable.

We had outrageous ideas when we wrote those little yellow stickies. One was asking a hundred friends to buy a hundred copies of *Chicken Soup for the Soul* to give away. It worked. Our friend Raymond Aaron, author of *Double Your Income Doing What You Love*, bought seventeen hundred books and gave one to each of his clients.

Our sales started by word of mouth. Each book had a pass-along value of five, so one reader earned us five more sales. We dreamed we could partner with Coca-Cola and Campbell Soup, and we did. We dreamed of our own TV show, and we got one on Pax TV. It all went into a business plan. They've all come true and more.

The same is true for you. Get to writing your goals.

The Bible says, "Thou shalt also decree a thing, and it shall be established unto thee" (Job 22:28). That means definite certainty. You have definite certainty the minute you put your thought down in writing. You're announcing the future right here, right now, by putting it on paper or in your computer.

Be flexible with your time frames. You set the 101 goals. Some are easy, some are hard; some you're more prepared to achieve right here and right now; others take time. Don't you dare lose faith. The late evangelist Robert Schuller used to say, "God's delays aren't God's denials." People may say that your goals are unrealistic, but everything's unrealistic. Car, telephones, planes, wireless communication, and computers were once unrealistic too. Nothing is realistic until it is realized.

Two of the best goal setters I've met were George Karr and Bob Barth, who led Equitable Advisors life insurance sales from their Philadelphia offices. Each of them had a personal and corporate monthly goal, succinctly and completely outlined, written in front of them in a Lucite block that sat in the center of their desks.

In the same fashion, the late Ben Feldman, considered the world's greatest insurance salesman, personally sold nearly two-thirds of all the policies that came in the door at the great New York Life Insurance Company. Each night Ben wrote down the names of ten people he would see and sell the following day. He also wrote the amounts he would be selling to each one. Why? Because he knew that his subconscious mind never slept and that thought projections were already moving out ahead and doing the selling for him. In his opinion, all he did was meet the people and finalize the agreements.

Ben always hit the amount he would sell, although he might miss selling person number seven and person number nine. This guy was such a superstar that he sold more in one year than 1,500 of the 1,800 life insurance companies, and that's why *Fortune Magazine* put him on the cover as the world's greatest salesman.

One day at lunch, Ben told me that people could earn $100,000 a year by working 250 days and earning $400 a day. A person who earns $1 million a year working 250 days earns $4,000 a day. The difference, Ben told me, was only one zero to move you from a six-figure to a seven-figure earning. Not bad, huh? Just think: one zero makes you somebody who can earn a million dollars a year.

W. Clement Stone, the billionaire, philanthropist, and business tycoon, said, "You figure out how much you can earn in a year; say that's $100,000. Once you know how to make a hundred grand a year, you squeeze it down into a month. Now you make a hundred grand a month. Now you squeeze it down to a week: you make a hundred grand in a week. Now you squeeze it down into a day: you make a hundred grand in a day. Then you figure out how to make a hundred grand an hour, and then in a minute."

If They Can, You Can

Obviously, people like Ben Feldman, Bill Gates, Michael Dell, Michael Eisner, and Steven Spielberg have all done that. Here's the deal: if they can do it, you can do it. They set a goal and got it, so you can set a goal and get it. Many of the goals that I have now obtained didn't even seem possible when I wrote them down. If it becomes your goal, you can do it. If anyone else in your industry or profession has done it, it's doable and therefore replicable. If it hasn't been done yet in your industry, find a similar industry where it has been done; then modify, adapt, or adopt what's workable and make it work for you.

You've got to have a positive mindset to move from ordinary to extraordinary. I give you permission to achieve greatness and success. Your obligation is to accept it, rehearse it, believe it, and achieve it. Also affirm to yourself daily, "I'm entitled to success and achievement."

As a matter of fact, let me give you a bonus idea. When you go to bed tonight, as you go to sleep, say, "I'm entitled to success and achievement. I'm entitled to success and achievement." If you say this a few hundred times, pretty soon it's branded into your brain, etched into the fabric of your being, and it's going to be yours as a truth about yourself. You're entitled to greatness. Make this your mantra until it becomes a truth about you and the truth for you.

If you're not yet a millionaire, I'd like you to be. It is necessary first to cultivate a millionaire's mindset. The quickest, easiest way to do it is write on a three by five card, "I'm on schedule to be a millionaire by December 31 of X year." Don't give yourself more than five years. Read that affirmation out loud four times a day with feeling and belief. Your subconscious gradually comes to believe it and ultimately will achieve it. It seems simplistic and perhaps even silly, yet when you consistently and persistently think about it, it'll come about. Why not become rich?

When are you going to read this statement? Four times a day: at breakfast, lunch, dinner, and most importantly, before you go to sleep, because your subconscious never sleeps. If you're saying, "I'm on schedule to become a millionaire," your eighty-six billion brain cells start to impress that idea and express it.

At first, you're going to reject this idea and say, "This is the dumbest thing I've ever heard," but just float with it. Try it. Give it twenty-one to thirty days, and you'll see that it works. You'll be elated, surprised, and reverently thankful. You'll wonder why someone somewhere along the way didn't tell you sooner. It's never too late. At the age of sixty-seven, Grandma Moses woke up to her painting ability and painted until she died at age 101. Imagine if she'd started at age seven or seventeen.

Stop Stalling

Stop stalling. Embed a big desire in your soul. Big desires keep your heart and soul on fire. Your fire is fanned by your dreams, ambition, dream team, and compelling lectures, books, audios, videos, and stories. You'll know you're here to serve and make a difference.

Once you've got your big desire, you'll come up against challenges, detours, and sidetracks, but understand this: nothing and no one can stop you but you. The average person gets the excitement and passion to expand their ideas and then shuts down. Once they start to explore it and figure out how to make it bigger, all the reasons start coming down the pike, saying, "No, you can't do that: that's already been done. How are you going to compete with Bill Gates or some of the other big people out there?"

My friend, that's the beginning of the end. That's self-defeating behavior. Don't listen to the dream stealers—especially the ones in your head.

There are two levels of obstacles: mental and real. Mental obstacles are those that you put on yourself. I once met a man who said to me, "I hate my job, but in eight years, I'll retire and be free." Wow. That's what I call a mental obstacle. I wouldn't want to do something I hated for eight seconds, much less eight years.

I can't imagine working at something that I hated. This is dysfunctional behavior.

Real obstacles show up when you go out into the workplace. People, money, resources, talents, clients, customers, all sorts of things seem to work against you at times. Let's face it: the amount of time you have on earth is limited. It doesn't matter what the mental or the real obstacles are. It's time here and now to set your goals, plan your big thinking, and live bigger than you ever thought you could.

Throughout history, only individuals who use their mind power beneficially have preserved their gains. Study Jesus Christ. The gains during his lifetime were infinitesimal, but look what's happened over the last twenty centuries because of his words. The size of your thinking determines the size of your results.

How to Be a Successful Failure

Research shows that you can be a successful failure. All you need to do is gossip, sneer about other people, and go on about what's not working, why the weather is against you, or why politics is slowing you down. You can complain, "I'd do it if it weren't for my parents, if it weren't for my boss, if it weren't for my spouse"—whatever or whomever you choose to blame. None of this is true. Every one of us can have excuses, but the choice here is, either have excuses or get results. Let's think big and go for big results.

You can be stalled by holding grudges, but this is dysfunctional behavior to the max. You can also be stalled by imagining your need rather than your vision. You've got to have a vision that's so big, so compelling, that it absorbs you into it. You have the vision, and the vision has you.

Another means of stalling is to project your lack of self-love onto someone else. You've got to have healthy self-esteem; you need to affirm yourself: "I love *me* positively and correctly, and I'll go forward and succeed."

Stop these bad mental habits for twenty-one days, and you're going to be a big-time winner.

Think Healthy Thoughts

In the game of life, you're the audience you're playing to. Even if you listen to the advice of others, in the end you are the person in charge of making your own decisions. Be daring enough to follow your dreams, to immerse yourself in them, and you'll find courage and boldness to achieve them.

The world respects people who can create. Just remember that in order to create anything, we must first dream it. To live your dream, you must first have a dream to live. Dreams create the world of reality. This chapter was first a dream. The words you're reading were first thoughts in my mind. With my computer, pen, and paper, I wrote down all my thoughts, ideas, hopes, dreams, and aspirations. (In fact, those very writing instruments were once someone else's dream. They were created and have been continually used to help make people's dreams come true.) In turn, I can help you make your dreams come true, so that you can help untold others realize their dreams. See your dreams. Your dreams can change an entire world.

Do you understand now that your thoughts can change your very being? That's why you've got to think healthy thoughts. Become fascinated with the ideas of health—become a student of what makes you healthy.

Most people don't know how to think healthy thoughts.

Say to yourself fifty times a day, "I'm healthy. I'm healthy. I'm healthy." It affects you at a quantum, invisible, subcellular level. Talking to yourself helps create your own good health cellularly.

The highest thing you can say to yourself is a prayer: "God in me is my health, right here and right now." Both psychology and physiology teach that all pain is in the brain. The mind can only think one thought at a time, even if it's got several thoughts in rapid sequence. As you program your mind to believe in health, you'll achieve health.

When I got amoebic dysentery in India, a neighborhood guru came to visit me at my sickbed. He hypnotized me to believe that I could take the pain, raise it two inches above my stomach, and feel it no more. I desperately wanted to be out of pain, so I did it. It worked. I can't promise it'll work for you, because I don't know your situation and circumstance. But even if it works half the time, wouldn't that be marvelous?

Your thought form controls trillions of cells in your body, which are changing at a rate of seven million cells a second. The law of polarity says you are always constantly regenerating or degenerating. You can only think pain or pleasure; you can only move toward or away from health. I want you to move towards it. Let's keep your body healthy.

Five Quick Tips

Allow me to give five quick tips that are absolutely necessary to your life.

1. Exercise every day, seven days a week. Oprah Winfrey says if you're over forty years old, you need an hour and a half of exercise. Whether you're male or female, you've got to be cross-training: do some muscle training and some aerobics. You can watch Orpah's videos and read her books on this.

2. Eat fresh fruits and vegetables. It fuels your body with rocket fuel to ensure high, vibrant levels of energy. You aren't necessarily what you eat, but you are what you absorb. Try eating five to seven fresh fruits and vegetables every day. It'll energize your system, mind, and body.

The goal is to be fully, vitally alive all the time and have energy to spare. Who's going to succeed more, somebody who's high-energy or low-energy? I suggest that will be somebody who has high energy, so you should be in that quadrant of people. Richard Restak, author of *Think Smart: A Neuroscientist's Prescription for Improving Your Brain's Performance*, says, "Brain functioning depends very much on what you've eaten for breakfast."

3. Herbs have a very specific purpose: to detoxify and rejuvenate your body. I've spent over twelve hundred hours studying the health benefits of herbs. I don't know everything, but I do know a lot. I've interviewed Dr. Gordon Patterson, one of the world's foremost students on herbal formulations and what they mean for your health.

I've also interviewed Dr. Brian Carpenter, who tells you how to eradicate 85 percent of disease, which starts in the colon. Herbs can prevent and sometimes stop the foremost killers of humans—heart disease and strokes, cancer, diabetes, and arthritis—because they detoxify your trillions of cells and allow your enzymes to nourish and rebuild your body from the inside out.

4. This is a great health idea, and I'm going to let it sneak up on you. I was in Puerto Vallarta, Mexico, having dinner with some great friends who also happen to be clients: Deborah and Doug Jones. Deborah leaned in and says, "Look, our son, Andrew, has a colon that won't work. He can't go to the bathroom. His mind doesn't tell him when to go to the bathroom. Every once in a while, he has an accident, which ruins him at school. He's only six years old. We've spent untold thousands going to the best doctors, but we can't get this kid's colon to work, and we just don't know what to do. He's got what they call a lazy colon." Andrew was going to the bathroom about once every ten days. It was causing many other health aberrations: he was told he had ADD and was slow, none of which was true.

I was so excited that I came out of my seat. I said, "Look, we've got this stuff called Life Fiber. It's got twenty-nine different kinds of herbs, both soluble and insoluble, and it gets the colon working again. The average person doesn't have enough fiber in their colon to make it work in an effective way. I tell you what: this stuff will work."

They said, "We've tried everything. We'll try this."

They brought Andrew over to my room, and I mixed a glass for myself and drank it because I thought he wanted to see the experiment. He smelled it and it didn't smell bad, so he drank some at once.

The next morning, Andrew came running up to me, saying that it worked. He went from being totally constipated to having a colon that went back into high-level work. His grades went straight up. His friendships went straight up. His self-respect went straight up, and his self-esteem was back where it was supposed to be. Deborah became a crusader for this product. I'm a crusader for it, because I know what it means to be constipated.

Eighty-five percent of Americans are so stressed out that they're full of it. According to holistic health pioneer Dr. Bernard Jensen, 85 percent of all disease has to do with colon problems. We exercise too little, sit too much, and don't ingest enough soluble and insoluble fiber.

Please listen to this with an open mind: check yourself by checking your stool. There are four Fs that you have to look for. If you have fawn-colored, fluffy floaters that are a foot long and have relatively no smell, your colon is really healthy. Otherwise your system is putting everything you ingest into a holding pattern, and that's dangerous. I'm not trying to offend you; I'm trying to educate you. Probably no one has ever discussed the state of your colon with you.

5. Stay off the three whites: white sugar, white salt, and white flour. White sugar causes sugar blues. White salt is prevalent in many foods for taste and as a preservative, but our body can't handle too much. White flour has had all the nutritive value taken out of it. Today's fast foods, which are loaded with the three whites, are harmful to the body.

If you don't input good food now, you're going to pay a big price down the road. After all, what use is there in living your dream or reaching your goals if you've poisoned your body from the inside out? Strategic coach Dan Sullivan says, "In the beginning, we trade our health for wealth. Later on, we trade all of our wealth just to get a little bit more health."

No One Else Can Give You Your Goals

Procrastination takes its toll on success and happiness; accomplishment and indecisiveness are as contradictory as success and procrastination. Your life will only improve by your actions. After I was turned upside down and bankrupt for months at age twenty-six, I had a classic case of inertia. I slept in a sleeping bag in someone's hall-way and ate peanut butter and jelly sandwiches until my tongue stuck to the roof of my mouth. I drove a beat-up Volkswagen whose wipers wouldn't work, and I'd say to myself, "If I wait long enough, maybe all this will work itself out." For months, I waited for things to get better; they only got worse.

One day I found myself unloading toilet paper from a railroad car in Long Island for $2.14 an hour. I said, "Mark, it's time to do something about this. I've got to get better, to make my life better. It starts inside my head, mind, heart, and soul." That's when that recording by Cavett Robert fell into my hands, and it worked for me. Can it work for anyone else? Absolutely.

It all starts with you. Jim Carrey was a nobody. He lived in Toronto with his parents, who were nobodies. Jim wrote himself an imaginary check for $10 million. He wrote in the memo section, "For great acting," showed it to his dad, and put it in his wallet.

Jim's first check, for a movie called *The Mask*, was $10 million. The day he got the job, his dad died. At his dad's funeral, Jim took his self-written check for $10 million out of his wallet, put it in his dad's hand, and buried it with him. He said, "You believed in me when no one else did." As he closed the coffin lid, he was overheard to say, "Dad, we did it." Jim Carrey couldn't wait any longer, so he took his life's plan in his own hands.

Walt Disney said, "If you can dream it, you can do it." No one can start your dreaming except you. And absolutely no one can stop your dreaming.

It doesn't matter that you're unemployed. It doesn't matter that you've got a dead-end job or are in a low-level position. It doesn't matter that you're a janitor. The Bible says, "For as [a man] thinketh in his heart, so is he" (Proverbs 23:7). Your thinking makes itself, and we're teaching you to dream big, live big, think big, and get bigger results than you ever thought you could.

4

Discover Your Genius

It's time to discover that the mind is within us and that it governs all we could possibly want.

There are two levels of mind: God's mind and our mind. The more our mind approaches God's mind, the more effortlessly we create. The Bible says, "According to your faith be it unto you" (Matthew 9:29). In lay language, what you believe is what you achieve. Hell and suffering can never be imposed upon us unless we impose them on ourselves. By the same token, joy, love, peace, happiness, and magnificence can't be imposed upon us unless we impose them on ourselves. Indeed nothing can be imposed on us unless we impose it on ourselves. Spirit can give no gift that we don't give ourselves permission to accept.

My friend, Dr. Michael Beckwith at Agape International Spiritual Center in LA, says, "Believe the truth about yourself, no matter how magnificent it is."

It's all in your head. It's in your head that genius begins. Mind power is only good when we recognize that it is *our* power. There's no more life in an ant than an elephant; it's simply spirit taking infinite forms. You choose your form, and then you become the form. Fortunately, we as glorious humans are entitled to greater good because we can conceive of greater good. Because we're capable of that, we owe it to God to follow through. The cliché says, "God gave you the gift of mind power, but what you do with it is your gift to God." I want your gift to God to be using your infinite genius potential.

If one of the smartest men of recent generations had lived a hundred years ago, no one would have known about him, because he couldn't walk or talk. Yet the late Stephen Hawking, the British physicist, cosmologist, and theorist on the origins of the universe, was, according to the scientific community, the smartest man since Einstein. He wrote a book called *A Brief History of Time*. This man communicated by typing with one finger into a computer on his electric wheelchair, which voice-recorded his thinking. (How many bona fide geniuses throughout history have we lost because we didn't have the tools to recognize them?)

Until Stephen was able to apply certain tools in his life, he was an undiscovered genius. He may have even died that way if the people around him hadn't understood how much greatness he carried in him and if the technology hadn't been there to help him communicate.

You're an undiscovered genius, too. In this chapter we're going to expand the six inches between your ears. As Oliver Wendell Holmes Sr. said, "A man's mind is stretched by a new idea or sensation, and never shrinks back to its former dimensions." Buckminster Fuller said, "All children are born geniuses, and we spend the first six years of their lives degeniusing them."

What Energizes You?

Find your genius. Find your uniqueness. Ask yourself, what do I like? What energizes me? What would I do if I didn't have to work? What's my passion? What's my unique calling? What's my life assignment? Discover what you're good at doing and what you're great at doing? Repeat it, improve it, polish it, grow forward and you'll wow yourself. The late Mary Kay Ash of Mary Kay Cosmetics told me that each morning she arrived early to work to put together a list of her day's seven priorities, and then she did them. That's how she built one of the most successful network marketing companies in the world. She knew what she had to do, and even more importantly, she knew what she was best at doing herself.

The quickest way to kill your genius is not to believe in your greatness. By saying silly things like, "I'm a loser.

I'm an idiot. I never can do anything right." Killing your genius ideas won't get you anywhere either. A lot of people come up with good ideas and concepts, which they then discount: "If that's such a good idea, somebody else would have thought of it already." "No one has done this before me, so I'm sure it's impossible." Or, "It won't work." How do you know?

Decide to become consistently exceptional. Create a can-do attitude to give yourself an attitude of gratitude—an attitude that's going to give you more altitude than anyone's ever had before. Maintain a positive mental attitude and an extraordinary mindset.

Understand that you're entitled to greatness and genius; you're entitled to have it all. Recognize that you cause your thoughts, and they're your servants. Therefore daily claim, "I'm a genius, I'm wise, I'm awake, I'm alive, I'm enthusiastic, I'm turned on to the infinite. If anyone else can do it, I can do it."

You have to learn how to unleash your creativity. How does a person tune in and turn on their creativity? There are people out there who believe they don't have a creative bone in their bodies. As a result of listening to these ideas, whether they came from parents, teachers, or themselves, these people don't reward their lives with meaningful purpose.

You can learn how to live and think outside the box. Success, prestige, recognition, and renown will all be yours. Thinking outside the box is a bridge to a whole new level of life. Heads will turn when you walk into the room; your presence will naturally and automatically command attention with no effort on your part. You'll partner with total self-confidence and leave your fears on the sidelines.

Be Your Biggest Self

I give you permission to be a bigger self than your old little self. Everyone wants to be their bigger self. No one wants to be doing or having the same old same old. The law of life is to grow, develop, improve, evolve, and become ever more and ever better. Study other geniuses to realize the genius in you. If you want to think out of the box, start studying the people who already think out of the box. Make sure you have access to a library of books, recordings, and articles by these geniuses.

The power you need to leverage yourself to the next level is information and knowledge, wisely and correctly applied. A real, deep education is self-education. When you are self-educated, you're hungry to learn from everyone and everything and everywhere. You're committed to lifelong learning. You can't get enough. You're an information sponge, drinking deeply of all the available wisdom.

If you can't afford to start your own collection of books and recordings, begin by borrowing from your local library, church, or like-minded achievement-oriented person. Visit bookstores and start building; eventually you'll have a library available to you right in your own home or office.

Jim Rohn says, "Just the act of walking into a library of your own makes you feel smarter and wiser." As you read and listen to other's concepts, you'll begin to have a few new ideas of your own. Some of us see our own gifts sooner than others. Some gifts at first may not look like gifts at all. We may be completely missing that genius.

Sparky the Loser

Let me tell you about Sparky as an example. For Sparky, school was all but impossible. He failed at every subject in the eighth grade, he flunked physics in high school, he flunked Latin, algebra, and English. He didn't do much better in sports. Although he did manage to make the school's golf team, he promptly lost the only important match of the season. There was a consolation match. He lost that too.

Throughout his youth, Sparky was socially awkward. He was not actually disliked by their students; no one cared that much. He was astonished if a classmate ever said hello to him outside of school hours. There's no way to tell how he might have done with dating because

Sparky never once asked a girl to go out in high school. He was too afraid of being turned down.

Sparky was a proverbial loser. He, his classmates, and everyone knew it, so he rolled with it. Sparky had made up his mind early in life that if things were meant to work out, they would. Otherwise he would contend himself with what appeared to be inevitable mediocrity.

One thing was important to Sparky: drawing. He was proud of his artwork. Of course, no one else appreciated it. In his senior year of high school, he submitted some of his cartoons to the editors of the yearbook, which were promptly turned down. After completing high school, he wrote a letter to Disney Studios. He was told to send samples of his artwork. The subject for a cartoon was suggested. Sparky drew the proposed cartoons, submitted them, and they were promptly turned down. Another loss for the loser.

Sparky decided to write his own autobiography in cartoons. He described his childhood self, a little boy loser, a chronic underachiever. The cartoon character would soon become famous worldwide. Sparky, the boy who had such a lack of success in school and whose work was rejected again and again, has a famous name now. It's Charles Schulz. He created *Peanuts*, the cartoon strip, and a little cartoon character whose kite would never fly and who never succeeded in kicking a football. His name was Charlie Brown.

Born Overendowed

You have undiscovered genius just waiting for the right stimulus. As you stir this awakened genius in you, you'll use it, and you'll begin to see it in others. Dr. Jean Houston says, "You aren't born endowed, you are born overendowed." If each of us were to encourage the genius in just one other person, eventually the entire world would work for 100 percent of humanity. Glenn Doman, author of *Teach Your Baby to Read*, says "Nature has built the brain in such a way that during the first six years of life, it can take in information at an overwhelming rate and without the slightest effort."

Every child at birth has greater potential intelligence than Leonardo da Vinci ever used. Before you can help others, you've got to help yourself. You got to find it in yourself and be wowed by it. Edison believed in his genius and invented the light bulb. If just 10 percent of the world's 7.87 billion people believed in their personal genius, eventually we'd get 787 million inventions equivalent to the light bulb. Talk about the world being well lit!

Speaking of well-lit ideas, I was having lunch with Jim Rohn when he hit me with an illuminating idea. When someone has a million-dollar home, where do the million dollars go? Who gets it? The bank, the architect, the contractor, the subcontractors, the laborers, the owner?

The million dollars is actually in flow. The velocity of money keeps moving through the economy until somebody gets scared and puts it in a holding pattern; then it's called a recession. Otherwise, the money is on the move, energy flowing instantly and constantly.

Big Thinkers Were Born That Way

It's amazingly difficult to get people to zero in on the fact that every one of them is a big thinker. The problem is most of us aren't born anywhere close to that kind of mind expansiveness.

John Newton was born in London in 1725. His mother died when he was seven. At age eleven, with two years of schooling and only a rudimentary education in Latin, John went to sea with his father. His life at sea was filled with wonderful escapades and a sailor's recklessness. He lost his soul in search of money, power, and pleasure, and eventually grew into a godless, self-centered, abandoned man. Eventually he was flogged as a deserter from the navy, and for fifteen months lived half-starved and ill-treated as a slave in Africa. His chance reading of a book entitled *The Imitation of Christ* sowed the seed of his conversion. Over the next six years (during which he commanded a slave ship), his faith matured.

John Newton spent the next nine years in Liverpool, studying Hebrew and Greek. He was eventually ordained and wrote hymns that are still famous. Who could know that a former slave and slave trader would be enough genius to write what has become the best-known inspirational song of all time, "Amazing Grace"? He once was lost, but now he's found. Every single one of us can be found.

Let me tell you another short story about a boy who was considered anything but a genius. He started out as a difficult, hyperactive child. Only music would calm him down. In school, he never applied himself, barely making it through any courses but music and history. Fortunately, his astute parents—his father, a professor of music, and his mother, a music teacher—stood up for their independently minded son. With their support for his real love for history, he was able to get into Oxford University, despite all his other failings.

Before this young man left home for school, he received a note from a young gas station attendant named Tim Rice. Rice claimed to be a with-it lyricist and wanted to partner with this young man's music. They became fast friends and dream team partners.

But off to college this young man went, to waste more time, not succeeding with anything but creating and composing his own music. He dropped out, and still his parents supported him. His first attempt at pop songs and musicals were unsuccessful. But he and Rice kept imagining and working toward their goal of making the charts with their music.

Out of the blue, they received a call from Alan Doggett, head of the music department of a British public school. He was looking for a concert for the end of the school term—something with a religious theme that would morally uplift the audience.

The inspiration resulted in a musical, *Joseph and His Amazing Technicolor Dreamcoat*, based on a story in the book of Genesis. Andrew Lloyd Webber and Tim Rice went on to write *Jesus Christ Superstar, Cats,* and *Evita.* Andrew Lloyd Webber went on from there by himself to create *Phantom of the Opera, Starlight Express, Aspects of Love,* and *Sunset Boulevard.* This high-school failure and college dropout presold $16 million in tickets for the opening night of the show *Phantom of the Opera* on Broadway. He's been knighted and been given a Hollywood star. (Let me put in a personal note. I've seen *Phantom of the Opera* in London, New York, Toronto, and LA. If you haven't seen *Phantom*, you haven't been to a play.)

Eight Levels of Intelligence

A Harvard professor named Howard Gardner wrote a book called *Multiple Intelligences.* His research shows that every one of us has at least one great talent that we could take to genius level if we work on it hard enough and sculpt it well enough. It's like the story in which someone asked Michelangelo, "How did you make your *David*?" He said, "I chipped out everything that wasn't David." Chip out everything that isn't your greatest genius, your greatest ability, your unique talent, which you can take to the pedestal of exalted genius.

Howard Gardner discovered that there are eight levels of intelligence. One is musical, like that of Andrew Lloyd Webber. There's athletic genius, like that of Michael Jordan. There's interpersonal genius, which has to do with sensing the emotions of others. Somebody with this type of intelligence could be a great salesperson, promoter, leader, visionary, or maybe a counselor or therapist. Other forms of intelligence include natural (understanding living things and relating to nature); spatial (visualizing the world in three dimensions); linguistic (finding the right words to express exactly what you mean); intrapersonal (understanding yourself and what you feel); logical-mathematical (quantifying); and musical (discerning pitch, tone, rhythm, and timbre).

In America, we have 37,000 kinds of occupations. In every occupation, there's probably one who's best, one that everybody else would call a genius. Why don't you become that person? In the book business, Jack Canfield and I have sold more books faster than anyone in history. We've decided to exhibit our genius in writing and speaking, and in my case, promoting and marketing and selling.

Everyone's got genius. I'm asking you to follow that great admonition, "Seek and you shall find." It doesn't say that some of us get to seek, some of us can find; it says all of us can seek, and all of us can find. But if you don't know to seek for your genius, you can't find it. I want you, from a spiritual, mental, and physical point of view, to seek out and find your genius and then manifest it, so that everybody can bask in the sunlight of your greatness.

Multiple Geniuses

Here's the secret. This is the magic of your soul. You've got multiple geniuses within you. After watching Muhammad Ali fight Chuck Wepner, Sylvester Stallone was so inspired that he wrote the movie *Rocky* in three days and three nights nonstop. He refused investors' money until he was promised the lead role, and then the movie went on to earn $100 million and win many Academy Awards. It spawned sequels that had sequels. It encouraged Sly Stallone to participate in several other movies, many of which, like *Rambo*, were multimillion-dollar hits.

Sly exhibited genius at writing a salable movie script. He exhibited further genius at selling it. Sly mastered the genius of being a bankable movie star. He became a savvy art collector and also became an artist. His artwork has been auctioned at record-selling prices that are usually only commanded by the Old masters.

When I was in Paris, my publisher and I were walking down the street about 5:30 at night. We walked by Sotheby's Gallery. The who's who in the world were traipsing in in their minks and limos, dropping off Old Masters to sell.

For my whole life, I'd wanted to go to Sotheby's.

We were in casual clothes, and we walked in between two prestigious groups. I just pointed as if we were with them. I mimicked a little bit of German, indicating that we couldn't speak English, and we got in.

Once inside, we saw all the Monets, Renoirs, and Cézannes, but whose pictures were selling for equally high prices? Sly Stallone's.

I believe each of us has multiple geniuses. We need to work one genius to greatness and then let our skills overflow and overgrow. Work your genius. The more you work it, the more you'll have to work with.

We Are the World

Ken Kragen is a kingmaker of show business personalities, a TV producer, a talent advisor, and a world-class fundraiser. Ken has transformed the celebrity lives that he's touched. He's also written a great book, which I'd love for you to read, called *Life Is a Contact Sport*.

Ken teaches that in order to make one big thing happen, three smaller events have to happen in a concentrated period of time. You have to start with big moves that are innovative and bold and have breakthrough potential. The three questions Ken asks are: Are the events something unique or special? Are they founded in real substance? Do they capture people's imagination or attention? If the answer is yes to all three, your career will leap forward.

Let me tell you about three events that came together for Kenny to create one big event back in 1985. First, his best friend, Harry Belafonte, called him after watching the horrific film footage of famine in Ethiopia on the news. He was convinced that American artists could do a charity event and give the proceeds to this cause.

Ken said, "Let's take Bob Geldof's idea for Band Aid, an all-star recording session, and do something bigger with it, with American artists." He called Kenny Rogers first, who loved the idea. He then drove over to Lionel Richie's house; it turned out that he'd also seen the news report about the tragedy in Africa. Ken asked Lionel to write a song with Stevie Wonder, and he'd line up the stars to sing it.

Simultaneously, Ken caught Quincy Jones en route to Hawaii for a vacation. Quincy Jones was totally over-worked, exhausted, and about to produce his first movie, *The Color Purple*, with Steven Spielberg. Nonetheless, he agreed to do the record, but he wanted to bring Michael Jackson into the project.

Then there was a second event. Within thirty-six hours, Ken Kragen called back Belafonte with the news: Stevie Wonder was occupied with writing songs for the film *The Woman in Red*, so Lionel and Michael wrote "We Are the World," and it was produced by Quincy Jones.

Kenny spent every waking moment talking to managers, agents, artists, lawyers, and record company publicists to make "We Are the World" a great success. His goal was to get two artists a day to say yes to this recording. He hoped for a total of fifteen, but instead twenty-eight knocked on his door, and he had to cut the line there. That was the third event.

Quincy was a perfect producer. He gave each artist his or her part so there'd be no question or jockeying for position. He posted a giant sign saying, "Hang all your egos on the door."

"We Are the World" was an impossible task that had perfect timing. It was put together in thirty-eight days. Deadlines forced instant action. Leaders came up with pioneering ways to feed the hungry. MTV devoted Saturday and Sunday to "We Are the World," and HBO ran a two-hour special on the making of the record and the video. Again, we had three events: radio, MTV, and HBO.

After that project, Kenny conceived the idea of Hands across America, a transcontinental human chain involving 6.5 million people to raise money for charity. What were the benefits Kenny received? He got more beneficial, high-powered contacts, more professional rapport, and more personal gratification than he'd ever received before.

What's Stopping You?

People all over the world are making it big in the world right now. What in the world are you claiming is stopping you, and why are you letting it?

When the 1984 Olympics were moved to Los Angeles at the last minute because the Ayatollah Khomeini had taken over Iran, LA mayor Tom Bradley looked around for the best turnaround guy on the planet and called Peter Ueberroth to explain the issue at hand. Peter asked, "What are you going to pay me?" To which Mayor Bradley responded, "$1," and he pulled it out of his pocket and gave it to him.

Peter needed $2 million to make the Olympics work, and in one week, he had it. He asked all the biggest companies to vie for position. He pitted Pepsi-Cola against Coca-Cola. He pitted Fuji Film against Kodak Film, and whoever came up with the money first, got it. It always pays to take action.

Every Labor Day for forty-five years, comedian Jerry Lewis had a telethon during which he stayed awake for forty-eight hours to raise money for multiple sclerosis. He raised millions and millions of dollars and stimulated new research efforts toward stopping this disease.

Starting in the 1940s, Bob Hope did trips abroad to entertain U.S. troops. It gave Bob and his team immense visibility, boosting our fighting soldiers' morale and providing unforgettable memories.

Milton Hershey founded the American candy bar company of that name in 1894. When he died in 1948, his personal fortune consisted mostly of his house and its furnishings: he had given the rest away. His chocolate factory employed eight thousand people through the Depression, and his workers enjoyed the good life at Hershey amusement park, lakes, theater, and bakeries. Milton Hershey and his wife created a school and orphanage for kids because they couldn't have any children of their own.

Let me close with a quote from my favorite genius of all time: Buckminster Fuller. I worked for him as research assistant at Southern Illinois University. I wouldn't be where I am today if it weren't for his input in my life. He received hundreds of accommodations and awards for his inventions and creative thought processes. He told me once, "I do it because I don't belong to me. I belong to the universe."

True genius isn't just for yourself. It's a responsibility, a rare true gift to the world. Seek out that greatness, that genius, in you, and make yourself count for something.

5

Challenge Your Challenges

If your life is lacking or if you feel like you've been attending the school of hard knocks, here's great news for you: you're moving on to greener pastures. In this chapter, I'll show you exactly how to get out of any rut you might be in, obliterate all your obstacles, and recognize that most problems are opportunities in disguise. Then I'll show you how to plan your days more efficiently and effectively in order to multiply, magnify, and magnetize your greater, grander, higher, and bigger self.

Input and Output Messages

We have to start where most of your obstacles lie—in your head. I call these your input/output messages. Many people stop dreaming because they've been bombarded with failure messages. We often stab our spirits to death by talking to ourselves with negative, killing affirmations.

Failure messages have been in most of us since we were young. As children, we heard things like, "Why are you so stupid?" "Can't you tie your shoes yet?" "Stop dreaming. The world doesn't work that way." "Why can't you be like everyone else?" As we grew older, we heard, "Settle down and make a living. You have a degree now, so don't mess it up. Don't rock the boat. Stop dreaming and get serious. What will other people think?"

As I said earlier, my partner and friend Jack Canfield is a self-esteem research expert and author of the all-time best seller *101 Ways to Build Self-Esteem*. Jack believes that just about everybody has good self-esteem up to kindergarten. By the time they graduate from high school, that self-esteem is down to about 5 percent of what it was, because most of it has been squashed out of them.

Your entire life is built on your self-image, what I call your "I am-age." What you add "I am" to, you become instantly and constantly. Your success is directly linked to your thoughts about yourself.

Research tells us that our self-image is generally incomplete and inaccurate. Think about that for the moment and what a loss that is. After years and years of wrong messaging, a good number of people don't believe they deserve to be successful because they've lost sight of their grander self.

You'll hear people say, "I don't have a family. I don't have a college degree. I'm overqualified. I'm too fat. I'm too skinny. I'm too ugly. I'm too cute; no one takes me seriously." If you let yourself listen to disaster messages, your life will become a disaster. Some people refuse to listen to or believe those heart-wrenching messages and go from youth to adult fulfilling dreams every step of the way.

Hit "Cancel"

Unfortunately, that's the rarity. When you first start working on thinking bigger, you have to stop these disaster messages in their tracks every time they start to surface. Tell yourself, "Cancel, cancel. Sweep it away." If you're into physical action, take your hands, make a big X, and say, "Cancel, cancel. Sweep it away." Or if you're with somebody and don't want them to see you do this, just use your little index finger, make an X, and say, "Cancel, cancel. Sweep it away."

Thinking bigger can make you a target for disaster messages from your family, coworkers, friends, and even total strangers. Not everyone will understand why or be happy for you. Most people like and accept the status quo, even if it's painful, but it's your choice whether you want to listen or not. You're going to have plenty of reasons to quit—everyone does—but you have a choice. You can believe in their reasons or you can ignore them.

Be careful, too, of other people's disaster messages seeping into your life. The evening news alone reports hundreds of these. No wonder so many people stop thinking big or stop thinking at all. There's no reason to allow these negative items into your life. Taking care of your own life and raising a family can be an overwhelming task. Focus on your life, your priorities, your bottom line for success, and hold that image in your mind.

Seventeen Ways to Subvert Success

Let's talk about why people don't think big. I believe there are seventeen reasons why people self-talk themselves out of success. I want you to understand these so that you could recognize them early, should they ever show up in your life.

1. They get negatively paranoid. Now you can be positively paranoid. W. Clement Stone said, "I'm a reverse paranoid. I think everybody's out to benefit me." That's how I want you to think. I want you to affirm that everybody out there is trying to help you. You need to kick the negative paranoia—"I won't be allowed to do it"—out of your mind.

2. Most people are satisfied with the same old, same old status quo. It takes too much energy to change things. But psychiatrists say, "We call people crazy who keep doing the same things and expect new results."

3. People waste energy and time regretting, criticizing, shaming, and blaming themselves or others for past mistakes and errors in judgment.

4. They have the wrong goals or low goals, or worse yet, no goals. If you have no goals, you can't fail, but you've got nowhere to go.

5. The doom and gloom experts in their lives have convinced them that they're incapable of winning.

6. They don't understand the laws of momentum and attraction, and they mistakenly decide to wait for easy money to come waltzing in the door.

7. People would rather be bored and secure than enthused and out there. An insightful quote from the cartoon philosopher Ziggy says, "Security is knowing what tomorrow will bring. Boredom is knowing what the day after tomorrow will bring." Security, no matter how boring, keeps people from moving on from a job where they feel stuck or unable to grow personally. Security has made them afraid of rocking the boat to work on relationships, walk away from relationships, or work through personal problems or phobias.

8. They feel they don't deserve success, especially if it has to do with increased money. For thousands of years, the prevailing thought of poverty has penetrated our thinking. That's bunk. Poverty just produces more poverty. Prosperity thinking produces rich, generous results. What you create and accomplish with your

money is most important. A long-standing belief in poverty as a virtue is more social than scriptural. As Dr. Frederick J. Eikerenkoetter (better known as Reverend Ike) said, "You don't have to go through hell to get to heaven." Your life purpose is to discover and use your God-given talents to make your existence on earth successful, healthy, joyful, peaceful, prosperous, and happy. You can accumulate wealth by helping others make their lives better. Your life is not a dress rehearsal. You're in the sweet here and now; you're already in eternity. Why not decide that you deserve and desire eternal happiness now?

9. They don't have a dream team, a network of big-thinking people that are like-minded, dependable, and trustworthy, and who see more in them than they see in themselves.

10. They're waiting for permission. Some people feel they aren't worthy to excel until they find permission or approval from others. Being alive is all the permission you need to succeed. Stop looking around and judging others as more deserving of success than you. If you're alive, you're entitled, period, but let me go one step further. If you need permission, remember, Mark Victor Hansen is giving you official permission to be a big-time winner, a big-time success. You're in charge of you starting right here and right now.

11. They aren't harvesting the gold from their people network. Flip through your contacts and determine who can help you realize your dream. Dreams are not achieved alone. Even if you work for yourself, isolated in your own office, you must have contact with other people in order to accomplish your goals. You need to have a constantly expanding list of people that you want to meet. Make that list now.

12. They stop after an initial success because they don't have a true grasp of what success is and what it isn't. Just because you've accomplished one success doesn't mean you have permission to quit. Use each success to go on to the next success. That's why you want to have multiple goals.

13. They use lack as a reason to not think big. "I'm too tired." "I'm too broke." "I'm too busy." "I'm not smart enough." They sound like Eeyore in *Winnie-the-Pooh*, who's always dragging his feet.

14. It's easier to be critical of others than take action for oneself. Motivational speaker Zig Ziglar once said, "No one ever built a statue to a critic, but boy, we sure listen to him, don't we?" Everyone's got critics. The bigger you get, the bigger your critics get, because a bigger target you are.

15. They're too busy living their life for others and putting off their own happiness.

16. Some people love to wallow in misery and don't want to change. When you think bigger, you lose sympathy from others. You're no longer able to feel sorry for yourself, and you've replaced the anxiety of failure with the adrenalin rush of conquest.

17. By refusing to think big, they don't have to deal with the responsibilities of personal success. On that same note, people on their way to having everything they want will invariably have to deal with situations that will feel new and uncomfortable. It could be exciting or terrifying, either a high or a low emotionally. If it's a low, it could make people freeze in their tracks.

Buying into Your Greatness

Now just in case you've recognized yourself in the obstacles above, I want to assure you that you can obliterate each and every one of them and step up to being one of the greatest thinkers in the world. If not you, who? If not now, why not? You've got a great, sharp mind or you wouldn't be reading this book. Stay where you are and you're cheating yourself, your family, and your world of your greatness. Everybody loses if you're underoperating, if you're living below your privilege.

Think of what would happen to *Rocky* if Sylvester Stallone had listened to all the failure messages. *Rocky* inspired our nation. It won Oscars for Best Picture and Best Director. Audiences everywhere cheered Rocky's triumph over the odds, all because Sly came out swinging with heart, soul, passion, humor, strength, and all his power turned on. My favorite line in the movie comes from Rocky's coach, played by Burgess Meredith: "To be a champion, you've got to eat lightning and crap thunder." Now that's clear, purposeful, and passionate.

Your success is directly linked to your thoughts about yourself. You will act out who you think you really are. You'll take on what you believe you can handle. Are you eating lightning and crapping thunder? Your own thinking is the only thing that can hold you back from what you want. It's time to think bigger about yourself, bigger about your world, bigger about your future. The people who believe they're prone to success will find a way to bring success into their lives. They'll attract it. They become success-prone, and they'll tend to succeed. I'm talking to you about *you*.

Obstacles Are Opportunities

Obstacles are opportunities in disguise. As you work toward success, you'll find that some obstacles are mental, involving self-talk and negative input from others. Other obstacles are actually real. They happen after you've contrived your dreams and go out to hear other people say no. Or you need the money, or you need to have a joint venture partner.

I believe all obstacles can be obliterated by applying motivation and imagination, which lead to momentum. Every experience of life is meant to strengthen your ability to motivate yourself. Each time you do, your momentum increases. Building belief and faith in yourself is a foundation that moves you forward regardless of any obstacle.

Country singer Garth Brooks wanted to beat the Beatles by selling a hundred million albums. It wasn't easy, but he did it. To his staff's surprise, he called them together, gave them each an advance payment for the next two years, and told them, "You're all on vacation, starting now. See you in two years." Garth, a ceaseless goal setter, went on vacation and then began to play baseball with the San Diego Padres, write rock music, and go on to star in a film. Now that's a life worth living.

Whoopi Goldberg was a San Diego single parent on welfare. She put together an improv act and went on the road. Two years later, at age thirty, Whoopi had a one-woman Broadway hit and the lead in the Spielberg movie *The Color Purple*.

Nelson Mandela served twenty-seven years in South Africa's Robben Island Prison for his belief in racial equality. The jailing of Mandela put pressure on the government to end apartheid and release him. After his release, Mandela was elected president of South Africa. Can you imagine hanging out in the slammer for twenty-seven years, standing on principle? That's why the world knows him, loves him, respects him, appreciates, and admires him, and he'll be one of the all-time greats in history.

Let me give you just one more example. In 1995, when America's Superman Christopher Reeves was thrown from his horse, he was left paralyzed from the neck down. The doctors told him it was for life. Chris wanted to die to stop the pain and the suffering his family would have to go through, until his three-year-old son crawled onto his chest, kissed him, and said, "Daddy, I love you, and I need you." He went on to survive and thrive. With his wife, Dana, at his side, Chris participated in extensive daily physical therapy to keep his muscles strong. Before his death in 2004, he lobbied for spinal cord injury research, including human embryonic stem cell research, and for better insurance coverage for the disabled. For my money, he really was a Superman.

Every savvy leader and thinker in our world today is a master problem solver. They all realize every problem has a price, and they go after their goals anyway, because they also know that every problem is an opportunity to give back something and make the world a better place.

The Example of Armand Hammer

In his book *The World of Armand Hammer*, John Bryson introduces us to a phenomenal can-do thinker. In 1921, at age twenty-three, fresh out of medical school, Armand sold his pharmaceutical company for $2 million. Russia had just gone through World War I, the Russian Revolution, and a subsequent civil war. Armand heard that the Russian people were suffering. He purchased $175,000 in medical equipment and supplies and went off to Russia.

Thinking he had prepared himself for human suffering during his medical schooling, Armand was shocked to witness the aftermath of war. Starving children had become skin and bones. The clothing of the dead was removed and handed to people waiting to reuse it. Mothers and fathers cannibalized family members just to stay alive.

As he traveled, Armand discovered that the Russians had plenty of material goods but no one to sell them and no distribution method in place. At that time, American grain was selling for $1 a bushel. Armand told the Russians, "I have $1 million. I'll buy a million bushels of grain and send it over. As each ship come in, load it with something that I could sell to pay me back."

The Russian leaders were shocked but appreciative. Later that year, when Armand returned to Russia, the Soviet leader V. I. Lenin met him personally and suggested that Hammer be the first foreign businessman to do business with Soviet Russia.

Armand agreed. He went on to become one of the wealthiest and best-connected men in the world. Lenin said to Armand, "We don't need doctors. We need businessmen." Armand got thirty-four major concessions, not the least of which was importing Ford tractors into Russia so they could improve their agriculture.

Employ Your Day for Greatness

The question you're sitting there asking yourself is, how can I do what they did? Armand could have gone home completely overwhelmed. Instead, he took one step at a time in the right direction, then another, then another.

I urge you to do the same. When you feel overwhelmed by your challenges, decide to live your life five minutes at a time. Instead of thinking about your long-range and sometimes overwhelming plans ahead, just focus on the next five minutes. Use that time to do the things that will bring you satisfaction and fulfillment and will advance you towards your goal. Each minute you use working on yourself goes out and works exponentially for you.

How do you transfer that wise use of five minutes to an entire day? Our success depends on how we use our time. Out of each day, we must create happiness, health, money, friendships, and spiritual evolution, rekindle our soul, and increase our mental abilities. It can be done in one day, every day, but it takes the right use of your time.

The next practical application is to employ your day for greatness. Everyone wakes up in the morning as rich in time as the richest, wisest, happiest person on earth. We all have twenty-four hours. What we do with them makes the difference.

Time has more value than money. Do you doubt me? Ask a father who has only hours to live. His children may be young and growing, and he will not get to see them through school. Ask him if time is more valuable than money.

Time is an hourly miracle. You wake up in the morning, and there it is. It's up to you to decide what you want to do with this twenty-four-hour building block of the universe. No one can take your hours from you; they're all yours. Everyone receives the same amount of time. Success is never awarded with an extra hour at the end of the day. You don't even lose your time if you squander it. To go into debt with time is impossible. You cannot waste tomorrow today. You can only use the present moment in the way that you see fit. Cavett Robert once said, "Killing time isn't a crime. It's murder."

Your life depends on making the right use of your time.

How does a person use the same twenty-four hours to go from being time-poor to having time freedom? By using your spare moments correctly. Often those neglected spare moments change your life for the better. Telegraph operator Thomas Edison used his spare moments for dreaming about and creating inventions that he later patented and made millions from.

Use your spare moments to create. The mind does well when challenged with a change of pace. It craves stimulation. Start thinking bigger now. No matter how well you feel your life is going, it could be better. While others are enjoying only a small portion of their potential, you can think bigger and live in ecstasy. Every moment that you use instead of wasting adds to the potential for awesomeness in your life. What about that ten minutes in the morning that some people spend reading the paper? Could you spend it gaining knowledge or working toward your goals? What about the time you invest exercising? You could be listening to audio recordings while you're out running or walking or bicycling and be rewarded twice. How about the ride home from work? If you're the driver, listen to audios. If you're the passenger, read books, write out your goals, plans, and strategies. How about the evening? Do you watch sitcoms? How about using that time to further improve your life?

The Ten Biggest Time Wasters

While we're on this subject, allow me to mention what I consider to be the ten most colossal time wasters.

1. Meaningless relationships that you don't analyze, decide, and extricate yourself from. You become like the people you hang out with, so in order to keep getting better, you want to hang out with people better than you. If you're the biggest hot dog in your social group, then you're a real weenie.

2. Living below your privilege. This happens when you don't think through your possibilities. Set great and inspiring goals, and live totally on purpose.

3. Letting time control you rather than being in control of your time. Write down what you want to do and the amount of time you're going to give it. Parkinson's law says, "Work expands to fill the time allotted to it."

4. Taking every single phone call rather than scheduling conference calls in advance and having a file with the notes and material you want to cover.

5. Overcommitting yourself and forgetting the value of saying, "No, not right now. If things change, I'll call you back."

6. Being underfunded, which slows you down and stifles your creativity.

7. Working in a dead-end job instead of taking a fast track to your dream job, your perfect right livelihood. A dead-end job sucks the life force out of your soul.

8. Experiencing almost constant low energy because of lack of desire and ambition.

9. Living out and fulfilling other people's dreams and goals instead of your own.

10. Watching mindless, brainless television. I'm not against TV. There's great TV, TV that'll exalt your spirit and catalyze you to greatness. TV is the center of your home entertainment. Because 87 percent of your mind is visually oriented, the TV absorbs you, and once you go into it, it goes into you. Look at your programming in advance, code it to the shows that you want, and then watch those shows in a prioritized fashion, but be judicious.

When my kids were little and I had total control, they got to watch only two hours of TV a week. My wife and I picked the best TV, the TV that would stimulate their minds to greatness, so that they would relish good thinking. Today they remain very judicious about what they watch.

You can decide right now what you're going to watch. Don't let the TV own you. Many people are unconscious: they go home, they turn the set on, and they vaporize many good hours while somebody else is making a fortune entertaining them. The person who kills time is also killing their potential. The person who is to succeed makes every moment count and come alive with full potential.

Take Time to Recharge

There's a big difference between killing time and taking time to recharge your batteries. When you don't take time to recharge, you're really no better off than people who are just killing time. You have too much potential and creativity to let it drain away.

People believe that once you've achieved a certain level of success, every day will go much more smoothly. You tell yourself, "Someday I'm going to be successful. Life's going to get better. I won't ever have to be anxious again."

I can tell you that even the most successful people have daily challenges: even the most successful can stay positive only for a certain period of time. We all need to continually recharge our batteries.

You've got to plug in and recharge to continue the full utilization of your mind. My colleague and friend Dan Sullivan says there are three kinds of time: (1) Work time: you spend 80 percent of your time earning money and doing all the activities required by your lifestyle. (2) Cleanup time, when you clean up your messes—family messes, financial messes, spiritual messes, social messes, family messes. You've got to reorganize in order to lighten your load. It gets the monkey off your back and reduces your stress. (3) Rejuvenation time, time to refresh and be reinvigorated. Dan says that you've got to have a twenty-four-hour period, midnight to midnight, with no business calls, business reading, or interruptions from anyone but yourself. Don't think or talk about business. Do your hobby or some other activity that distracts you from business. Then you'll come back rejuvenated. You'll be new again.

You'll then find that out of the ten problems that you had been facing, seven or eight will have vaporized automatically. The other three you'll handle with courage, *élan vital*, *savoir faire*—you'll click through them, just like that.

Your ability to keep your battery positively charged will increase your self-confidence, and as your self-confidence increases, you too will increase in every good way. When you want to recharge, use audios, books, seminars, movies, your dream team, and only positive friends.

I used to hike the Appalachian Trail with a dentist friend and his family. Dr. Jimmy Webber would always say, "We're almost there. It's only a little farther." Even when we were really only halfway through this grueling climb, Dr. Webber's cheerleading encouragement always worked. It's the kind of influence you need in order to keep going.

As you make your daily and weekly plan, you have to schedule downtime. All of us need more downtime. In the old days, you'd work six days and take one off. Most people did manual labor then, but today many of us are in the thinking business, and if you're in the thinking business, the more free time you need.

Research proves that fact. For every week you take away from your usual business activity, you'll return refreshed, and you'll have one breakthrough idea. Two separate free weeks will guarantee two major breakthroughs in your business and life. Funny how it works, isn't it? But it does work. Every single month now, I take off one week, and business is better than ever.

Each minute you use working on yourself goes out and works exponentially for you. You'll begin to reap rewards faster than you'll know how to accept them. In the next chapter, I'm going to talk about unlimited opportunities, and you are going to learn how to see with new eyes. You'll discover that there are more opportunities than you could ever harvest.

6

See Your Unlimited Opportunities

As I traveled around the world, I've seen money-making opportunities that I never suspected. When I was in Malaysia, someone drove me by the biggest home estate in Kuala Lumpur. It was owned by the gentleman who made the Visa and MasterCard franchise happen in his country. I never knew such a deal existed. I share that with you because as you read business periodicals like *Success Magazine, Forbes, Fortune, Inc., Entrepreneur,* and *Selling Power,* consider the possibility of taking over a franchise in your city, state, or region. With warp-speed travel on the horizon and virtual business here already, your geographical whereabouts become ever less import-ant. If you have key connections, associates, or interests, it is really that simple. H. L. Hunt was one of the first oil billionaires from Texas. When asked how one becomes a billionaire, he put it simply: (1) Decide what you want. (2) Decide what you have to sacrifice to get it. (3) Set your mind to it and do it.

We have gone from the depth of the Depression in the 1930s to the height of expression, just like in the Renaissance. During the time, no one knew that they were in the Renaissance. Even today, most people don't recognize the immense opportunities and powers we have right here at hand. Why is it so extraordinary now? The industrial economy is now powered by the virtual economy—the Internet and the digital revolution, which is infinite, fast-moving, and unstoppable. Catch this concept.

Once you're awake to big thinking, everything in life is an opportunity. We just need to be awake and use our heads and our senses to tune in, turn on, and see what's out there for us.

A Smile and a Shoeshine

I want to introduce you to the world's greatest shoe-shine person—Jill Wright. She's sparklingly effervescent. Her attitude is impeccably friendly, buoyant, optimistic, and helpful. Her family was made up of Dale Carnegie instructors, and everyone in the family learned how to have excellent human relations. She owns a shoeshine company, Executive Shine, at the airports in Denver and Charlotte, North Carolina. The Executive Shine website says, "By treating her teams well and always putting Love first in every interaction, [Jill] has some of the most loyal and dedicated professionals in the world working for her."

Jill says her clients are lonely, stressed out, and hassled, and need someone to talk to away from home. To get clients away from their humdrum attitudes, Jill says, "I get them to quickly change their focus from what's troubling them to subjects they enjoy talking about." She asks them for help. She says, "Look, I'm planning a vacation," and then asks them to describe them the best vacation they've ever experienced. In an instant, she has switched them from a mental pain to a new mental pleasure. Add the pleasure of having their feet rubbed through their shoes, and you can see how their energy will shift.

Jill knows and teaches her team the sage psychology of serving. She says, "My teammates who earn the most are masters at changing and redirecting the client's energy focus from negative to positive by talking pets, weather, sports, or business. I have respect for my clients and my staff. I treat them all like they want to be treated."

Jill's team has shined more than a million pairs of shoes. Most customers are repeat customers, because once they get an expert high-gloss shine, they want all their shoes to be radiant and glistening. Many people drop their shoes off for Jill and her team to shine. The owner of one company likes her so much that he sends his shoes in every week by FedEx with a FedEx return slip and payment in the shoes. That alone should tell you that Jill goes the extra mile with a smile and has great word-of-mouth.

Jill and her team put everyone in kinglike, cushy, comfortable chairs she bought from a hotel chain at $5 each and had reupholstered into ergonomic perfection. When you sit down, you know you're in for a treat. The team members only talk to the customer they're with while he or she sits in that chair. The team performs seven exact steps to an excellent shine, the likes of which are rarely seen in a modern-day shoeshine practice. One step is that she melts the polish in by passing a match over the shoe, so it soaks in; then she finishes with nylons to bring it to an extra high gloss.

Jill believes that people in a high-tech world love high touch on their feet. I'll bet she's the highest-paid shoeshine person on the planet. Her people are also the highest-earning shoeshine people anywhere, and she lets them keep up to 80 percent of their earnings. She's making more money than most CEOs. She loves her work, and she's proud of it. She enjoys befriending her clientele. And she's the only shoeshine person I know who collects bigger-than-average tips, a thank you from most, and more hugs of appreciation than anyone I've ever seen shining shoes. She's a well-loved entrepreneur who supplies massive value and is growing exponentially—there are airports to work at everywhere.

Now let's review this: Jill picked a business that she loves and that loves her. It didn't require any heavy start-up investment. It's a business anyone could do. Her opportunities are endless, just like yours when you start to think about them.

All growth comes from intellectually based service businesses. It's entrepreneurship versus bureaucracy. Once you've turned yourself into a professional services firm, no matter what you sell, you win.

The richest man of all time was an archetypal no-limit thinker named John D. Rockefeller Sr. Self-made giants like Rockefeller always fascinate us. Ron Chernow wrote a book about Rockefeller called *Titan*. I listened several times to this book on tape until I heard and felt the music of Rockefeller's mind. Chernow says, "Rockefeller embodied thrift, self-reliance, hard work, and unflagging enterprise." I got a picture of John D. as a real person who worked hard and saved more than 50 percent of all of his earnings and journalized every expense. He believed that opportunities were abounding and endlessly available for him and for anyone who worked hard, worked smart, and worked different. He did it; it worked. You can do it, and it'll work. Rockefeller's name graces buildings, monuments, libraries, and universities, notably Rockefeller Center in New York City, complete with winter skating rink. He wanted to make a big difference and leave a big legacy. He maximized his opportunities and pushed the

limit of what one human being could do. He's a phenomenal example of earning it, growing it, and giving it away.
All it took was being awake to the opportunity.

Don't Let Others' Mindsets Limit You

People who take very little action generally spend most
of their time criticizing. After all, they have plenty of
time for it. Have you ever noticed that people who go
after their dreams and goals have very little time to criticize others? They're too busy thinking and acting on
their own dreams and goals (otherwise called minding
their own business). Being a critic is easy. It requires no
effort or special education. Being a doer requires much
more of a person: courage, tenacity, uncertainty, and
willingness for transformation.

Critics are common. You'll find them everywhere and
anywhere. Doers are the rare heroes. Yet our society pays
a certain homage to its critics. They even pay to hear what
they have to say: movie critics, food critics, government
critics, business critics, sports critics. Why? Because it's
easier to criticize someone else's performance than it is
to go out there, be in the battlefield, and be the performer.
The mind defaults to the ugly.

It's easy for people to beat up on others. It's easier to
tear down than to build up. The real champions of the
world have zero time available for criticizing others.

Instead, they are busy living out their own dreams and leaving the critics in the dust.

Champions don't criticize other people. They help others strengthen their talents and become great too. Yes, there will be times when you look for constructive criticism, but only from trusted members of your dream team. (I'll talk about your dream team in chapter 8.) If you're listening to the criticism of people who are not in the trenches with you, or who do not have your best interest in mind, you're setting up yourself up for failure. Listen to criticism only from people who understand and support your dreams.

This is true even if you have family members who are criticizing you because they love you and don't want to see you hurt. If they don't fully understand your dreams, and if they haven't accomplished similar goals, don't listen to them. As harsh as it may sound, they have not earned the right to help you.

You must ignore the self-appointed critic. Forgive yourself and others for limitations of the past and move on. Spend your time seeking out the many people who have earned the right to help you.

Don't Limit Yourself

Now that you have the limiters out of your life, don't limit yourself. If you are infinite, your potential reaches beyond any experience that you've ever imagined; the only limitations are those that you impose on yourself. Being alive is the only permission you need to think bigger than you ever thought you could.

A person with one large Internet company approached a businessman and asked for the electronic rights to his information products. The businessman went to his lawyer and said, "No, they're not doing any electronic distribution of this. Tell the Internet company to cease and desist." The Internet company was simply proposing additional revenue streams for the businessman. Because electronic distribution was not part of the man's self-image, he went negative. At the time, that Internet company was getting 310 million hits a day, and the number has since grown.

The businessman just couldn't handle the idea of electronic media. Here was a gentleman who operates his business in the same old, same old way. He'd just put in $40 million in new equipment to support the same old way of doing business when it was time to expand in an unknown market.

Push yourself; strive to think bigger and think outside the box for other potential markets. Be open to possibilities instead of repelling these ideas out of fear. This man's only vision was, "I'm making $100 million a year, and I'm going to continue making $100 million. Why would you do anything else?" Yet his industry is changing, as is every industry. We're all heading towards electronic media and e-commerce. Instead of being open to a legitimate opportunity to play with some of Internet's biggest players, this man became paranoid and denied an opportunity that could have taken his income into the billions.

Understand this: you never stay in one place ever. You either make expansive decisions or contracting decisions. Which direction are you moving in?

An insurance agent was having a hard time making ends meet. He had an office and a staff, and their production was in a slump. He went to an industry consultant, who told him how much he would have to sell in order to make money: "Either expand the sales to make more money, or eliminate expenses."

The insurance agent said, "I'll do my own janitorial work. I'll spend one day a week doing janitorial work for seven people, so I don't have to pay for it; then I don't have to worry about expansion." He felt this made him safe. He didn't spend any more money on advertising, training, or additional efforts to increase his sales. But in reality, this insurance agent ruined his own business.

Self-Fulfilling Prophecies

Self-fulfilling prophecies could be positive or negative. To give you an idea of a positive self-fulfilling prophecy, consider the businessman who dreamed that someday he would lead the Boston Philharmonic Orchestra. His business was so profitable that he mustered his courage, hired the orchestra, invited all of his friends, took adequate tutelage, and performed successfully before more than two thousand people. The media ate it up. He became front-page news around the world.

Deep down, all of us want to realize our loftiest and most inspired desires. The only thing that really stops us is us.

Allow me to share one personal example. One of my six thousand goals (and I've hit 1,587 of them) was that I always wanted to go to a Hollywood party. Now I live in the LA area, so that should be easy, but I never got invited to one.

My wife and I get remarried every year: we write our own marital vows, and we get in front of ministers. I decided that if I couldn't get invited to a Hollywood party, I'd have one. One year we hired the Shirelles, and they sang their famous hit "Goin' to the Chapel" in front of five hundred friends and clients.

Amazingly, they'd brought a guest celebrity with them. Richard Street, the head of the Temptations, sang all of his songs. When he was reintroducing the Shirelles, he went into a Barry White voice and said, "And before the Supremes were the Shirelles," and the audience went wild.

Don't limit yourself. Figure out how to have so much financial wherewithal that you can pull off the real magic that you want. You may be tragic now, but tune it in and turn it on to be magic.

Develop Momentum

Once you get past the limiters and your own limiting thinking, how do you develop momentum in your quest? That part is easy. Many times each day, simply think about your desired goal. The more you want and believe in your goal, the stronger the power of attraction will be. When even a small event or sign goes your way, build momentum on top of momentum to get your emotions to follow your dreams, believe in your goals, and take action. Your feelings about your dreams and goals will follow your actions.

To feel even better about your dreams, talk and act enthusiastically about them. If you walk, talk, act, smell, feel, and look enthusiastic, guess what? You'll be enthusiastic. And enthusiasm's last letters are I-A-S-M: "I am sold myself." As Cavett Robert told me once, "When you're convinced, you're convincing."

You've got to attend seminars, you've got to listen to audios, you've got to be associated with big thinkers, and you've got to read positive, inspirational books. Jim Rohn says that you need to be reading two books a week. If you don't have that reading input, you can't have the through-put and the output. The quality of your input determines the quality of your output. I think I am able to have ideas upon ideas and be an idea merchant because I'm an omnivorous reader and an omnivorous listener. I'm a consumption machine of higher thinking.

There's Infinite Supply

Once you've mastered big thinking, you'll find there's an infinite supply to fill even the biggest demand. Why not expect something extraordinary to come your way? *USA Today* told about two art collectors in Lincoln, Nebraska, who paid $225 for a copy of a Monet and discovered it was an original. It was called *Boats on the Banks of Gennevilliers* and had been owned by a New York collector who sold it to an Omaha country club, and it hadn't surfaced for years. When Wayne Rankin and Fred Niemann went into the antique shop, they were told it was a copy. They figured it was worth at least $225, so they bought it. When they auctioned it on eBay, the top bid came in at $1.8 million.

Infinite supply means that if you have an eagle eye, you may find a great collector's piece of art and turn $200 into almost $2 million. If it can happen for somebody else, it can happen for you.

Joe Charbonneau began his career as a turkey farmer in Wisconsin but became the owner of one of the largest insurance companies in the Midwest by age twenty-four.

He has since built an international educational company with ninety-six audio and visual training titles.

Let me give you a little background on Joe. In 1981, he had 110 franchises throughout North America, Europe, and Africa. During that time, the interest rate shot up to 19–20 percent. His business went right down the tubes. He owned a ten-thousand-square-foot facility with office space, his own printing company, and high-speed cassette-duplicating system, and had people everywhere with lots of revenue flowing. Nonetheless, he found himself one day standing in an airport in Chicago waiting to go bankrupt. He had no money and didn't know which way to turn.

That's when Joe asked himself, "What can I do? I know our stuff is good. How can I help independent business-people stay afloat during this terrible crisis?" One of his clients was Ace Hardware. He decided to pay them a visit. At their meeting, he offered to sell his training series to the stores. The tape series sold for $500, and vendors could buy them wholesale for $250. He told his Ace Hardware contact that he would sell the tapes at $19.95 each and send the store one tape a month for twelve months with a price that guaranteed below wholesale. He thought he'd have to beg, but Ace Hardware said, "Great. Sounds good. When do we start?"

As Joe left Ace Hardware, he realized that True Value Hardware was actually a larger client for him than Ace.

He called the president of True Value, Dan Cotter, and explained what he had done. Dan said, "If you did it for them, you'd better do it for us." True Value had nine thousand stores. Joe was beginning to realize he had just stumbled onto a system. He went to American Hardware, and by the end of the day, he'd sold $1 million worth of tapes at $19.95 each. He had realized that people are interested in continuing their education, but they don't have enough time to attend classroom-style lectures. From that opportunity, he built the largest private-label training company in America.

William Shakespeare wrote, "All the life's a stage / And all the men and women merely players." Most of us can't tell prime players in our life from the minor walk-on roles. It's critical to discern the difference between the prime players, who can radically change your lives, and those who can't. Joe discovered the major players and built a giant business.

Sam Walton, the founder and creator of Walmart and Sam's Club, said, "The customer is king. They can fire anyone of us any time they don't like us and decide they don't want what we're selling. Therefore everyone at our company is in the customer service business every day of our lives."

Walton started in Bentonville, Arkansas, and built an ever-expanding operation, primarily in small-town U.S.A. and then in small towns worldwide. Sears thought he'd be a guppy in a retail pool, but Sam Walton had other ideas. He had a finger on the pulse of his clients. He was simply and quietly effective. As a result, he outthought Sears and everyone else and became the world's largest retailer.

Walton was first to embrace digital communications. He read nightly computerized reports of what was selling in high quantity at any store and immediately deployed the product throughout his chain. Because he could quickly move high quantities of merchandise, he received the lowest prices and often got goods on consignment. Walton was loyal to his customers, family, shareholders, and the Walmart team. He also understood them. As an example, people were afraid of security guards at the front of the store. Sam outfitted his security guards in street clothes with big smiles and had them operate as directory assistants to the customer. Theft declined, and goodwill increased on all sides.

Several points: As Sam Walton proved, if you can start in Bentonville, Arkansas; you can start anywhere. Second, it doesn't matter who's currently dominating the market. If you have a big, strong, compelling vision, you're going to succeed in a bigger way than anyone ever thought you could.

Third, new thinking, new ideas, new marketing applied to old models is always needed and always will win. Fourth, ambitious fast starters like Sam Walton always employ new technology. Fifth, when you think with your customer's interest in mind and build accordingly, you'll never fail.

Remember, opportunity is everywhere, so always stay awake to big thinking. In the next chapter, I'm going to show you just how far big thinking can go and where it's going to take you.

7

Innovation to Maximization

In this chapter, you'll learn about innovation to maximization. You can innovate by finding and filling a niche with a particular product, service, idea, benefit, or personality. Maybe you know a better way of running a business or can see the technological possibilities in our ever-expanding world.

Taking a good idea and making it better is a great way to innovate. I call it *plussing*, and it's a great way to use innovation to maximization. You can use innovation to maximize your ideas, your results, your benefits, and your success.

Jesus said, "Seek, and ye shall find" (Matthew 7:7). That means all the time, always, everywhere, by everyone. If you seek an idea—like a way to talk to the computer—you'll find an idea. Seek innovation and you'll find it, but innovation needn't be high-tech. Why not seek a simple innovation like dental floss or luggage pull carts? Someone sought out and found and cashed in on solutions like that, and so can you.

My late friend Art Linkletter, who hosted the TV show *People Are Funny*, saw the hula hoop when he visited Australia in the early fifties. He brought it to America, sold millions, and gave us a new form of exercise and entertainment.

Innovators love to imagine what is possible. One metaphor for the possible is Camelot, and in chapter 12 I'll discuss how we can realize the possibility of Camelot in today's world for everyone everywhere. Everyone needs to blast off into big, innovative thinking and prepare to realize the possibility of Camelot—the good life in their lives so that they and we can all have it.

President John F. Kennedy was a charismatic, idealistic realist who wanted to create his version of Camelot by saying, "Ask not what your country can do for you, but what you can do for your country." Paraphrased, I say, "Ask not what God or the world owes you, but what can you do to give back to God and the world, and all of our fellow human beings and all the other animals on the planet too."

Let's include everyone. President John F. Kennedy dreamed of creating Camelot during his presidency. Although he didn't use the term (Jacqueline Kennedy used it after his assassination), he spoke of it in almost every speech. He said, "In this decade, we will land a man on the moon." Kennedy personified innovation and possibility of thinking and action. He called out the best and the brightest. They came, rolled up their sleeves, engaged their thinking, and got swept up in the possibility of making history.

Why not create a life and lifestyle with substance and style? Why live below your privilege for even a nanosecond? The world in all its bounty is yours for the asking, the being, the doing, the thinking, and the having. Enjoy life and everything it has to offer to the max. If you don't have the means, decide to create the means. They are totally available when you believe you can live up to your privilege and help others to do the same.

The Power of De-Aging

The late Victor Borge was a consummate performer—an extraordinary comedian, pianist, and pantomimist. Born in Denmark and relocated to America, he delighted audiences around the world during his entire long career. Victor evoked mirth with his unforgettable antics, pratfalls, and musical brilliance, interlaced with superlative and surprising humor. He used his talents to help build a living Camelot out of his experience of life.

My wife and children and I reveled in watching Victor perform and transform on his eighty-ninth birthday, in 1998. We were lucky to have seats near the front so I could see the great Victor Borge in the curtain wings. He stood there looking old and arthritic, with a cane, and was being held up by an aide-de-camp.

When Victor was introduced, I witnessed an instant shapeshifting. He spontaneously lost thirty years of age before my eyes. His spine lost its rigidity. His countenance became radiant, happy, and joyous. He handed his cane to his aide-de-camp, and a spring miraculously came into his step. A lifetime of performing before kings, queens, presidents, princes, and us common folk had habituated him to a stature and a persuasive performance stance that was comfortable, though worn. His age vaporized. He was in his zone. He was doing what he loved and what God had coded his DNA and RNA to do.

Victor Borge was a unique, one-of-a-kind superstar, more than impressive. I watched him live countless times on television, and I brought others to join me in his good, clean, uplifting, joyous humor and style. I witnessed the remarkable transformation of a physical body. I share this story with you because it shows that aging and mortality are in your mind, soul, perception, and habits.

The work of Drs. Deepak Chopra and Ken Dychtwald prove that we can de-age. We can de-age in a blink of an eye as Victor Borge did, because an audience was depending on him to contribute to their laughter, love, and fulfillment. Victor Borge, Bob Hope, Buckminster Fuller, Dick

Clark—each in his own way continued to perform as they aged, not because they needed the money or the accolade but because it made their lives a Camelot realized; as they served, they felt needed, loved, important. The audience received the essence of their contribution and invariably gave them standing ovations. They also heard the words not spoken. As Ralph Waldo Emerson said, "Who you are speaks so loudly, I can't hear what you're saying."

These performers were saying, "Let me entertain you and edify you, soul to soul, heart to heart, core essence to core essence. Take who I am at my best. I cheerfully give you my all. Here's to my Holy Grail, my personal sword Excalibur. I hand it to you in love, appreciation, gratitude, and thanksgiving. I want to make a meaningful and memorable difference. And for this, I get to be, for one brief moment, a shapeshifter out of my old, degenerating, decaying, dilapidated body into a younger form. I am self-hypnotized into remembering for one brief moment my Fred Astaire movements of grace, joy, and youthful vitality. In my elder statesman role, I ask you who are aging to keep revitalizing and renewing your eternal youthfulness."

Early in my speaking career, I was hired by AT&T. The senior vice president told me that almost everyone in America had a phone, and they used it a few times a day; that was all there was to the phone business. He was an insufficiency thinker, limited in imagination and stuck in what was, not what could be. Since that time, we've seen dozens of types of phones developed. Smartphones, computer phones, Internet phones, video phones. They're ubiquitous, and they're helping to fuel the economy. That VP's attitude was exactly the opposite of innovation to maximization.

We're going into a Camelot-type time, and I for one am glad to be here. The creators of this world are the dreamers. Look around. What is visible to you now was first invisible, only a vision in the mind of its creator. Often dreamers and their visions are called foolish. Believe in your ideas. Believe in your visions. Believe in your dreams. Your dreams and your decisions are realities in your heart. You will someday experience them as reality on earth. What you dream you become: even life itself at one time was a dream, a hope. The butterfly waits hopefully in a cocoon. Parents dream of a new addition to their family. Your decisions, desires, and dreams are what you will someday experience. They are the seeds of your future.

People without dreams look at the accomplishments of those with dreams and call it luck or chance. The non-dreamers don't realize that the dreamers became the achievers long before the results were seen. They became the winners the minute they immersed themselves in their dreams before the rest of us saw the worldly evidence. The luck on the dreamers' side was really action. What they achieved was the direct result of the action they took. Life is a result of action based on your decisions, desires, and dreams.

The Bible says, "Faith is the substance of things hoped for, the evidence of things not seen" (Hebrews 11:1). Sounds like gobbledygook, but success is an inside job. It's visualizing, which you impress and will ultimately and inevitably express.

Most people dream of success, but success is a direction more than a destination. Success is a progressive realization of your dreams. There are many possibilities for you. There are opportunities out there; you just need to find them.

Where am I going to find these ideas? you ask yourself. Start by looking in your own industry and see which problems exist. Ask for problems; turn them into opportunities. Every person, every corporation, every association has problems. Problems all have price tags and somebody willing to pay to solve them. You might find yourself ahead of your times. Jack and I were; that's one reason we received 144 rejections for our first *Chicken Soup for the Soul* book.

The Danish poet Piet Hein wrote, "What the world needs now is problem solvers galore / because each problem we solve creates ten problems more." That means a lot of price tags available for you and me.

In 1913, the Russian composer Igor Stravinsky's ballet *The Rite of Spring* evoked laughter when it was first performed in Paris. The laughter became a riot as the audience protested against his style of music. Stravinsky, unruffled, continued the performance. Eventually the world came to regard *The Rite of Spring* as one of the masterpieces of the twentieth-century music, and they saw Stravinsky as a genius.

Stew's Secrets

Stew Leonard, a former milkman who saw his milk route evaporating before his eyes, decided to innovate to maximize by creating a grocery store that would be a wow of experience for customers. Today Stew has a fabulously successful grocery chain in Connecticut and upstate New York. *USA Today* listed it among the top ten retail groceries in America for 2020.

A sign in front of the store says, "Point 1: the customer is always right. Point 2: reread Point 1." He sees the lifelong value of his customers and teaches the same values to all of his employees. Stew says, "If a client comes in and buys $50 worth of groceries, and does that 50 weeks a year, that's $2,500. You treat somebody worth $2,500 a lot differently than somebody that's only worth $50. But if you multiply that times 50 years of customer service, you're now way over $100,000 of value per customer."

Stew goes on to say, "Look at every customer as if they've got a bag in their hand that says, 'I'm worth

$100,000 to you if you treat me, love me, like me, respect me, remember my name on a first-name basis, and be friendly to me. I'll keep coming back and buying from you. I'll do business with you forever.'" He gives great prizes for the most unusual places where Stew Leonard shopping bags are seen. Customers send in photos, which he hangs on the wall, puts in brochures, and gets in newspapers and on TV. People fly in helicopters and parachute out of airplanes with Stew Leonard bags. One guy climbed Mount Everest carrying a Stew Leonard bag and brought back the picture.

Stew asks all of his customers the questions you and I need to ask in our business: "What did we do right and what can we do better?" He asked one lady, "What did we do right, and what can we do better?" She said, "I'll tell you what you did right and what you can do better. You leave those shopping carts out here in Connecticut out in the rain. When I come here with my baby that's wearing a diaper, the baby sits in that little baby seat. That dry diaper sucks up all that wet. Then the baby's uncomfortable and cries all the way through the shopping center. I'll tell you what I want you to do, Stewie. I want you to have paper towels, I want you to have carts covered with wood, and I want to be able to wipe those carts off with paper towels so my baby doesn't have a wet bottom." Stew said, "In a million years, I never would have thought of that."

Another lady came to him and said, "Stew, I'll tell you what I want you to do. You always give us the strawberries in little bushels. The big, beautiful ones are on top, the squished ones are in the middle, and the squashed ones in the bottom. I'll tell you what I want you to do. I want you to wash and clean all the strawberries, lay them out, let me taste them, and then let me pick the ones that I want so I get only good strawberries."

When Stew brought that idea to his board of directors, they said, "You're nuts. They'll be eating all our strawberries right on the site." But his profit on strawberries went up 400 percent that week.

Stew keeps innovating to maximize his business, and everybody goes there. You could use these innovative ideas in your own business. Just keep asking everybody, "What did I do right, and what can I do better?"

Acres of Diamonds

The best ideas haven't been thought of yet. Look in your own industry. Turn problems into opportunities. Pastor and educator Russell Conwell gave a classic talk called "Acres of Diamonds," in which he said, "There are more acres of diamonds in the human mind that have ever been pulled out of the ground." He gave this great talk over five thousand times, generated over $6 million, and built Temple University in Philadelphia.

Years ago, a secretary heard Dr. Conwell give his famous speech. At that time, she was pinning papers together and kept pricking herself and bleeding on the papers. She said, "There's got to be an easier way to put papers together." Today, in downtown Philadelphia, right next to Temple University, there's a seven-story paper clip dedicated to that great woman's idea. She came to Conwell's talk, and she got the message. She found her diamond mine: the paper clip.

Find the diamond mine in your mind. It's in your backyard. It's hidden in plain sight. Look for ideas: you have fifty thousand ideas a day. All you need is one, and then maximize your innovation.

I believe everyone needs to write out their dreams and schemes and then keep on thinking about how they can make them come to pass. This idea is simple, and it works. I hope it stimulates you to conjure up new possibilities. When you have a great idea, you need to keep looking at it from every perspective and plussing it (my term for adding to it and making it grow).

When *Chicken Soup for the Soul* took off, we kept plussing it to make it better. We marketed horizontally with numbered books—a second helping, a third serving, a sixth bowl of chicken soup. We've vertically marketed new niches: *Chicken Soup for the Woman's Soul*, companion volumes for teens and preteens, for Christians and golfers.

The Bible says, "My cup runneth over" (Psalm 23:5). When you're doing good thinking, your cup's supposed to run over. My friend Jim Rohn said, "If your cup's not running over, it's because your cup's upside down."

You're born rich, as Bob Proctor says, with eighty-six billion brain cells. I'm here to tweak you, pinch you, goad you, and irk you to use this great thing that you've been passive about. I want you to think expansively and keep plussing your ideas.

You could even create an event and then sell it out. The Ironman triathlon was started in Kona, Hawaii, in 1978 to see what the height of human achievement could be. It is still held annually in different locations worldwide.

All it takes is just one new idea, a little turn, a little tweak. Each of us is one idea away from greatness. Raise your index finger, look at it, and say, "I'm one idea away from doing something innovative and creative to maximize my life and better the whole world." Give yourself a challenge for that one great idea.

If you're using my three by five card analysis, I want you to write down, "I've got a great multimillion or billion-dollar idea." Look at it four times a day: at breakfast, lunch, dinner, and bedtime. Percolate that thought through your brain cells for the next twenty-one days, and ideas will start to spill out. When you have them, write them down on a piece of paper, in your future diary or your journal, or put them into your computer.

As you look at those ideas, write down complementary ideas for realizing your main idea. Don't rush this process. Let it simmer. To your amazement, money, resources, needs, people will show up to help you realize your dreams. Never stop writing down ideas. They will wake you up and excite you with new possibilities.

When I met with Ray Bradbury, the great science fiction writer, I'd just read his classic novel *Fahrenheit 451*. He told me how it came about:

"I'm lying in bed, and I'm in deep sleep, and all of a sudden a fireman from *Fahrenheit 451* is shaking my foot. I woke up in a start, I got goosebumps, and I said, 'What do you want?'

"He said, 'Don't you want to know why I burn all the books?'

"'No, I don't think so. I want to stay asleep.'

"'Get up; go to your typewriter. I've got to do the rest of the story.'

"'Can I have a cup of coffee and go to the bathroom first?'

"'Nope. I've got to tell you the rest of the story.'" And Ray Bradbury went to his typewriter and wrote his next great book.

He may have meant this as a metaphor; nonetheless, when you've got ideas circulating and percolating in your mind, they've got to come out. They're going to wake you up. I usually wake up at four in the morning, because there are no disturbances and my mind is processing ideas.

This is going to happen for you, but be smart enough to grab those ideas, harvest them, and let them work for you. Whether it's filling a need or finding a solution in a business familiar to you or branching off in a whole new domain and creating multiple sources of income, you can use innovation to maximize your life, your love, your joy, your health, and your future. I look forward to hearing what you've done.

8

Dream Teaming

In this chapter, you will learn how to multiply your creative power and energy by creating your own dream team.

In its simplest sense, synergy is a concept whereby one plus one equals eleven, and sometimes much more. People working together can accomplish far more than they could ever accomplish working separately. Two or more people working together can unleash incredible power in what Napoleon Hill called "operating in the spirit of cooperative harmony."

I'm going to show you how to find and expand your true talents and natural abilities, how to attract people who want to help you succeed in your dream team, and how to cooperate rather than compete. You'll learn how to go through life feeling accepted, fearless, and successful. It's simple to multiply ideas into multiple successes.

You've got to have a dream team to fulfill your dream. You need at least one other person who can help you focus and share your purpose.

Andrew Carnegie coined the term "being on purpose." It means having a clear, central life goal. His life goal was to gain wealth by marketing and manufacturing steel. Once he had made his money, he went on to do the most good and least harm with his money. He said that he couldn't give it away fast enough. In his later years, Carnegie was worth $475 million, which would be $7.2 billion in today's dollars, but by the time of his death in 1919, he had given away all but $30 million.

Anyone who achieves noteworthy success or greatness as an artist, teacher, scientist, businessperson, preacher, or anything else must have a dream team. The dream team partner or partners may be visible, or they may be totally behind the scenes. That doesn't matter. What matters is that they're there.

Be All That You Can Be

Dream teams help you be all that you can be. We all have hidden talents and creative ideas. What abilities do you have? You may or may not even be aware of them. Often a person discounts his or her own talents. A dream team will uncover your abilities and help you to expand them.

Who would want to listen to me talk from the podium? Who'd want to read what I have to write? Who would trust me to help them plan their finances? What do I know?

All of us have self-deprecating statements; all of us have self-doubt. A dream team partner sees more in you than you see in yourself. Like the Ugly Duckling in Hans Christian Andersen's story, almost all of us have deflated self-concepts. We think we're unattractive or clumsy, socially inept or dull. We all need friends and those who love us to encourage us and nurture our strengths.

That's why you've got to find a Master Mind buddy who sees more in you than you see in yourself. He or she will cheer you on, root for you, encourage you. All of us need a Jiminy Cricket sitting on our shoulder saying, "You can do it. You can do it. You can do it."

At the same time, few people are willing to look at their habits. That's why you need a dream team: to show you the habits that need changing. If you change one habit in twenty-one days, over three years you can reinvent fifty-two habits. Write down the habits you want to change, and have somebody follow up with you.

As I witness religious dream teams like those around Benny Hinn, Michael Beckwith, Sai Baba outside Bangalore, India, or Dr. Paul Yonggi Cho in Seoul, Korea, I noticed each has a loving, faithful, committed membership that send them focused energy, which helps them to perform healings. That kind of combined energy is electric and intensive, and it works.

A Megamonster Retreat

One of the most fascinating Master Mind retreats in the world is hosted by Herbert Allen, CEO of an investment company called Allen & Company, which has had a hand in several large tech IPOs of the last decade, including Twitter, Groupon, and LinkedIn.

The Allen & Company meeting, held at Idaho's Sun Valley Resort, is confined to a single industry: communications. The participants are leaders of companies like Microsoft, Sony, Amazon, Dell Computer, Sprint, *The Washington Post*, ViacomCBS, and NBC.

Unlike other prestigious leadership retreats, it includes the entire families of these leaders. There are no sweaty, noisy bus rides to this retreat. Most of the hundreds of adult guests and children arrive by private jet. For five days, the guests enjoy a wide range of amenities, from fly fishing to white water rafting, from golf to massage.

It's not the recreation that draws some of those powerful business moguls in the world; it's the Master Mind sessions, the dream teaming, the synergy. Remember, *synergy* refers to a whole system that is greater than the sum of its parts. The retreat is five days of dream teaming among these individuals to make the world work better individually and collectively.

Major business deals have been orchestrated at this retreat. It was here over golf that Michael Eisner made his first pitch to buy CapCities/ABC, culminating three weeks later in a $19 billion acquisition.

Invitees here are kingmakers. Herb Allen clearly understands the power of dream teams. He's put together the finest minds in the communication field.

As a big thinker, you could create similar social functions, which could capture the minds, hearts, and attendance of the who's who in your group. Big moves happen when big thinkers get together, and somebody's got to create that retreat. Make it your goal, or at least one of your goals, to create a megamonster retreat that gets megamonster results. Why not? It's no harder to think big than to think small, but the payoff is vastly bigger.

The giant redwood trees in California are more than four thousand years old. They're a must-see. One is so large that it has a hole carved out that large trucks can drive through. If you inquire about how they have out-lived every other species of tree in the planet, you quickly discover that redwoods are a dream team. They are shallow-rooted and intertwined underground. They support each other through earthquakes, inclement weather, fire, and every other adversity.

Likewise, with a dream team, you can have it all and handle it all. Virtually underground, it can last forever. It can give you a potentially self-perpetuating legacy.

A Dream Team in India

When I was a student ambassador to India in 1968, I was paired with an aristocrat, Byron Tucker, from Amherst College. We seemingly had nothing in common. I was middle-class, and he was quite upper-class. Surprisingly, we became great friends and dream teamers. Between us, we could seemingly figure out how to master and conquer any situation. I'll give you two quick examples.

In 1968, India's men and women remained separated in public, even on railroad cars. The trains had open windows, and the men's cars tended to be dusty, dirty, and overcrowded. Byron suggested we ride with the ladies. Their train cars were practically empty and clean, and our cultural system seemed to OK it. On the first day, people came and said, "You can't sit there." We acted innocent and said, "Sprechen Sie Deutsch?" They obviously didn't. We sat tight, hurting no one, and rode in relatively luxurious comfort. It made a multiday train trip tolerable and enjoyable.

After our studies were completed, we chose to experience what's called the Big Diamond, visiting Bangalore, Madras, Calcutta, New Delhi, and then going back home through Bombay (as these cities were then called). We immersed ourselves in the culture and drank in every sight, sound, and nuance. It was a real education. We were alone and living by our wits. We had to constantly be on our mental toes.

Even though we were staying in youth hostels for virtually nothing, our funds eventually ran out. We were in Calcutta with three rupees—about 25 cents—between us. We had given or traded away all our American clothes and gifts. We had been living on bananas picked from the side of the road. Then Byron had a creative idea. He says, "Let's go to the maharaja's estate."

We jumped in a cab and raced out to an outrageously opulent and ornate palace. We paid the driver with the very last of our funds, and Byron told me quietly, "Just follow my lead."

The doorman, who spoke limited English, asked, "Are you senators, presidents, congressmen, and generals?" To each inquiry, we said, "No. We're experimenters." Unable to understand that terminology, he got the maharaja, who customarily met only with the British queen on the second floor of his palace, to come down. For us, he descended his hand-carved, white Carrara marble staircase. He must have weighed over four hundred pounds, and he had gleaming, bejeweled rings on all ten fingers. He warmly and smilingly greeted us with the namaste gesture, which means, "The spirit in me blesses the spirit in you."

Byron said, "General Smith, who stayed here during World War II, sends his love, friendship, and greetings, and asked us personally to give them to you."

The conversation was apparently working, as he invited us to meet his son and daughter, who were approximately our age and studied at Oxford. Within an hour, we were invited to be his house guests for the next two weeks.

What did you learn from this experience? First, anyone can use their best thinking and a dream team to come up with original and unusual solutions that make life interesting, worthwhile, important, and memorable. Second, instant solutions exist in dream teaming. You've got to have a pal. Providence makes us individually incomplete. You've got to have a partner to think with through situations and circumstances. Third, everyone can win and create valuable memories. Fourth, it's impossible to rise above your own vision. That's why you need a dream team with members who have unlimited vision. Until you find yourself with a limitless vision, hang around those who have one.

The Constitutional Dream Team

There are countless stories of people with limited abilities that have produced extraordinary results. The story of the U.S. Constitution is one of them. The United States of

America is one of the youngest nations on the earth and yet has the oldest constitution on the planet. From 1776 until today, the government of practically every other nation has changed, but ours has held steady.

One of the greatest accomplishments in government was the writing of the Constitution of the United States. Fifty-six men came together and declared independence from Great Britain, not because of their religion, blood ties, power, or wealth, but because, they believed, God had made them individual men who were endowed by their creator with certain inalienable rights, among them life, liberty, and the pursuit of happiness (and may I add, the happiness of pursuit). These individuals envisioned a great nation and worked together with their ideas to formulate a plan for the future. They dared to dream. Look at how our lives have been affected by that dream team.

Most people have far more potential than they realize. A dream team has a specific purpose—to help you focus on your goals. You can build an ad hoc dream team for specific needs, then disband or restructure the team as your needs change.

Keep in mind that not all dream teams focus on business goals. Some focus on relationships. A husband and wife dream team can be extremely effective. A home dream team, a husband and wife, join their heads and hearts to attain happiness and financial security. Marriage can be a perfect dream team, blending love, oneness of purpose, and sympathetic understanding in complete harmony. It is the highest of highs.

Brainstorming with Kids

A great way to think bigger is to brainstorm with kids, because kids don't know boundaries and don't worry about expense. Have kids in your dream team. Futurologist Faith Popcorn does. My friend, Mo Siegel, a cofounder of Celestial Seasonings Tea, says, "You've always got to have an eight-year-old on your board of directors. Eight-year-olds have a crap detector. They don't take any, and they don't give any."

When I heard Mo say that, I was making a promotional video for my speaking business. My daughter Melanie at that time was exactly eight years old. I already invested $20,000 in this promo video. I invited Melanie to come and edit it with me and paid her $50 to evaluate it.

The opening scene showed me in Newport Beach, California, standing next to a seven-foot, six-inch statue of John Wayne. She said, "Daddy, you need to have a little bullet coming out of his mouth that says, 'Hi, Mark.'" We added it, and everybody who watched it laughed and chortled.

We need to have kids. They know how to think big. They're intrinsically unlimited, self-actualized, fully functioning people.

Rodgers and Hammerstein

Richard Rodgers and Oscar Hammerstein II, pioneers of musical comedy, did not collaborate until they were well along in their careers. Hammerstein first met Rodgers after a Saturday matinee of a college varsity review. Like Rodgers, Hammerstein was keen to push the boundaries of the musical, which was only slightly more sophisticated than vaudeville.

The announcement that Rodgers and Hammerstein were to collaborate on a musical called *Oklahoma!* was initially greeted with skepticism. The financial backing proved very difficult to raise. The word from the tryout in New Haven, Connecticut, was awful. One of Walter Winchell's informants wired the columnist, "No girls, no legs, no jokes, no chance."

But on March 31, 1943, *Oklahoma* opened and triumphed on Broadway. The show began with a lone woman churning butter on stage to the strains of an off-stage voice singing, "Oh, what a beautiful morning." It captivated that first-night audience. This revolutionary music also changed the mainstream of the genre forever. Rodgers and Hammerstein wrote nine musicals together, this revolutionary musical changed the mainstream of the genre forever. It was made into a movie.

In 1957, when I was going back to Denmark with my parents, it took almost a half month to get from New York to Copenhagen by ship. The only movie they had was *Oklahoma!* I watched that every night, night in and night out. I know every one of these songs. Those two men made music that made your heart soar on the wings of lyrics.

After Hammerstein's death from cancer in 1960, Rodgers valiantly plowed on, but came to nothing. His melodies paled against his former output. Perhaps he no longer had the right partner to bring out the best in him. Most collaborators lacked Hammerstein's puritanical discipline. Sixty years later, the partnership of Rodgers and Hammerstein has not yet been equaled; it probably never will be.

The Team of Buffett and Munger

Warren Buffett, the richest investor in America, started with $100 and is now worth billions and billions. He claimed that his business really didn't take off until he partnered with a gentleman named Charlie Munger. Together they created the richest investment company ever, called Berkshire Hathaway. Like Herb Allen, they have meetings in Omaha, Nebraska, where both of them live, and the who's who of the world fly in to see those meetings. It's quite an event.

Think back in your childhood. Did you buddy up with another young person and accomplish anything, big or small? As a sixteen-year-old, I watched the Beatles and was inspired and wowed. In two weeks, I'd formed my own rock group, the Messengers.

Young, old, or anywhere in between, you can team up with somebody and do something great. Michael Jordan was arguably the best player ever in basketball, but he was well aware that he benefited from other players on the team. He said, "If I'd been born on an island, learned the game all by myself, and developed into the player I came to be without ever seeing another example, then yes, maybe I could accept being called the greatest, but I have used all the greatest players that came before me to improve my skills. I can't be called the greatest."

At one point Michael said, "If I'm going to have more games on than anyone else, I need this coach, Phil Jackson. I need this rebounder. Yeah, he has pink fingernails and he does his hair every night, but he's the greatest rebounder of all time." Michael picked his team to win. They were the best of the best. He set all of his records because he created his own dream team.

When Napoleon Hill was on his deathbed, he was asked if he had to pare down the thirteen principles in *Think and Grow Rich*, which ones he would choose. Hill said, "First, you've got to have a definite major purpose, and it's got to be in writing.

"Second, you've got to have a Master Mind group of two or more people working in a spirit of cooperative harmony for the attainment of a definite major purpose."

Putting Your Team Together

You may be asking, how do I choose my dream team? You have to have a compelling dream that everyone wants to realize. Failure to harmonize and sympathize causes the ruination of many businesses. Every mind in the group has to work together for a greater good. What counts is not the surface cooperation, but the in-depth agreement and the mental attitude of each team member. The heart and head must be in alliance and working with a leader to establish and maintain harmony. Moreover, each member has to have a definite motive behind all their actions.

We all operate through habit and motive. We start our actions by motive and keep doing them because of established habits. Hire the smartest and the best by being a student of the same. Be on the lookout for the best people; then propose the possibility of working together.

Remember, talent equals your future and your fortune. Who would your ideal dream team be? You need people who are trustworthy, dependable, motivated, happy, enthusiastic, and result-getting. Use your network to connect you to anyone you want. In the computer business, they say you're never more than six clicks away from anyone. You are never more than three people from whomever you want to meet.

I want you to vastly upgrade your dream team ideas in order to create and enjoy magic, miracles, and profound freedom. Help each member of your dream team to discover and maximize their unique talents. Hire for natural talent and extraordinary attitude. If someone on your dream team is negative, selfish, or egotistical toward the group, they clearly don't fit in.

That's why everyone needs to be put on a three-month probationary period. Mother Teresa insisted that all of the volunteers that came into her charity had to go on a three-month probation. She said, "Unless you exemplify the spirit of joy in contributing and seeing Christ in somebody else's eyes, you're out of here."

Mother Teresa was a great leader, and the leader of every dream team must be the first into work and usually the last to leave. They must always go the extra mile with a smile, making themselves indispensable, remembering that every leader's motto is, the greatest amongst you is servant of all.

Finally, there's one more important rule for dream teams: the relationship must be confidential. The best way to tell the world about your success is to show them your results. Let the group purpose be known only to the group, to you, and to God.

The Power of Agreement

Do these rules seem harsh? This is your life. This is your influence for life. What happens within your dream team affects not only you and the people involved but the entire world. Please don't take the selection process lightly.

Matthew 18:19 says, "If two of you shall agree on earth as touching any thing that they shall ask, it shall be done unto them." There are four definitions of agreement, it seems to me. The term could refer to agreement between you and God, between your consciousness and subconscious, or between you and another person—or it could be all three. I think the right answer is the last one: it's all three.

Andrew Carnegie once said that he knew little about manufacturing or marketing steel, but he did say, "I surround myself with more than a score of men whose combined education, experience, and ability give me the full benefit of all that has been known up to the present time about manufacturing and marketing steel. My job is to keep these men inspired with the desire to do the finest job possible."

Carnegie appropriated this principle of the Master Mind from the New Testament in the example of Christ and his twelve disciples. You recall Christ's unique powers and the powers of his disciples after he was crucified. Carnegie believed that Christ's power grew out of his relationship with God and his harmonious alliance with his disciples.

When Judas Iscariot broke faith with Christ, he experienced the supreme catastrophe: he lost his life. Likewise, when harmony in a dream team is disrupted, ruination follows.

Carnegie couldn't have gotten anywhere near the fame and fortune he experienced without his team. Nor could he have stayed at that level if that Master Mind had ever chosen to leave him. There are one-person businesses and industries, but they're not great. Their achievements are limited. Only dedicated, committed, directed dream teams enjoy the power of blended mind and the intangible force that no single mind can ever experience.

Two in agreement create greatness and manifest miracles. This power is available to you. If you don't have a dream team, write down as one of your goals, "I'm creating my own dream team," and see it come to pass.

9

Network!

This chapter is designed to help you become a competent, confident networker. You're going to learn twelve basic concepts that will enable you to achieve this goal.

I want you to have magnetic eye contact, an above average handshake, and a radiant presence, such that you go from business interaction to business interaction, relationship to relationship, gaining ever more success as you apply the principles in this chapter.

Please decide to become as rich as you can as a master networker. When your network grows, your net worth grows. These principles apply to sales, relationships, love, and life. They'll make your life richer, fuller, and ever more meaningful.

One of my colleagues has defined networking as a process of developing and nurturing contacts for four reasons: information, advice, support, and referrals. Former president George H. W. Bush was a masterful networker. The first person he called when war was breaking out with Saddam Hussein in 1990 was the British prime minister, Margaret Thatcher. Next, he went to Soviet leader Mikhail Gorbachev. That's world-class networking.

Gorbachev was also a master networker. I believe that he was one of the great men of the twentieth century. He had a network with the who's who of the world in an effective, nonthreatening, totally beneficial way. Gorbachev courageously ended the Cold War and befriended America. He took Russia out of communism. For those achievements, he's going to go down in history.

Believe me, you've got the same capacity too. That's the kind of networking I want you to do. I want you to make all the money and have all the friendships and relationships you need to accomplish your goals. I want you to go to higher principles and serve for the love of serving, care for the sake of caring, and sharing for the sake of sharing, knowing that it's going to come back to you in ways known and unknown. When you have a big list of contacts, everybody wins, and everyone's better off. As soon as you've got one networking contact or Master Mind partner, go on to the next and the next and the next.

Twelve Concepts of Networking

1. **Become an effective, result-generating master networker.** The late Robert Muller, former assistant secretary general of the United Nations, was a great writer, thinker, artist, and poet. He created twenty plans for peace while he was at the UN. Everybody said the plans were crazy, but he later said, "I kept talking about them, kept believing in them, kept cheering them on, kept selling them, kept promoting them. Now eighteen of them have been implemented."

One of Muller's projects was writing one idea-dream each day for nurturing a better world. He wrote over seven thousand idea-dreams. In his speeches he spoke of them and over the years noted that many of them were being worked on; some had been completed.

Here's an idea-dream for you: decide to network. Use every letter you write, every conversation you have, every meeting you attend to express your fundamental beliefs and dreams. Affirm to others a vision of the world that you want.

Network through thought, network through action, network through love, network through the spirit. You are the center of the network; you are the center of the world. You are a free and immensely powerful source of life and goodness. Affirm it, spread it, radiate it. Think day and night about it, and you will see miracles happen. The greatness of your life in a world of nearly eight billion individuals will lead to a new freedom, a new democracy, and a new form of happiness.

2. **Networkers are in high demand and low supply.** As an effective networker you become a valuable commodity.

As I've mentioned, Armand Hammer was a master networker. I suggest you that you read *Hammer: An Autobiography.* Back in the early 1920s, Hammer went straight from high school into medical school at Columbia. In his senior year as a medical student, he had to take over his father's pharmaceutical business. Hammer discovered that the plant was making money with a product called tincture of ginger, used at that time (during Prohibition) to make bootleg whiskey. Armand cornered the world market for tincture of ginger and made $2 million instantly while still a medical student. He ran the pharmaceutical company more or less during the day, studied at night, and graduated cum laude. As I've already pointed out, he went to Russia and, discovering that the people were starving to death, purchased a million dollars of wheat and started feeding the people.

Hammer used as many of his assets as he could to purchase Russian art treasures accumulated during the tsarist era and returned to New York at the height of the Great Depression. His brother said, "You're nuts. You're never going to make it now. You're trading in artwork at a time when no one has any money."

But Hammer had an idea for growing rich in his niche. He went to New York's Metropolitan Museum of Art and negotiated to do an art show for which he paid for the advertising and supplied the art; the museum supplied the facility. They charged people 50 cents apiece. Even during the Depression, people wanted to be entertained, and this was affordable entertainment, so they stood in long lines to see the Russian art treasures. Hammer got 25 cents, and the Met got 25 cents. In a very short period, he made $1 million, as more than four million visitors came to view these masterpieces.

Hammer was a medical doctor who became a salesman who became a businessman who became an entrepreneur who became a leader, an art collector, and a philanthropist. As I said, you've got multiple forms of genius. You need to discipline one, take it to the max, and then you will awaken the others in you.

Hammer became a visionary leader, a prototypical executive for the twenty-first century. Once he established his own business, Occidental Petroleum, he was forever expanding, because his mind kept expanding. He networked with great style, finesse, and competence. It's important to know who's the best and learn and glean from their methods. He's the picture of what you and I can become as master networkers.

3. **Networking is an art, a science, and a technology.** It's a way of life that is omnibeneficial. At one point, a young man named John Johnson was working in the mailroom at the Supreme Life Insurance Company in Chicago. He was a young whippersnapper, aggressive, with high aspiration and drive. One day, he was reading *Reader's Digest* and realized that black people made the covers of magazines only when they had done something wrong.

John realized that there were few good images for blacks out there and decided that the world needed a magazine for blacks. He talked to the chairman of the board, who happened to be black, and said, "Look, you've got thousands of insurance customers. Let me send out a direct mail piece and offer them a black digest for $2 each." Two thirds of the people who receives the mailings sent their money, saying, "Yes, I want a black digest."

Originally this publication was produced by the Supreme Life Insurance Company. Ultimately it became *Ebony* and *Jet* magazines. John Johnson ended up buying back the entire insurance company. Little ideas, well networked, have phenomenal results. If you haven't read his book *Succeeding against the Odds*, I promise you, it'll inspire you at the depth of your being.

Allow me just one little example from the book. When John F. Kennedy was running for president, he came to John Johnson and said, "Look, I want to be president of the United States. Twelve percent of our population is black. Most of them don't vote for anyone. You haven't got a black candidate running. I would like to be your candidate." John Johnson interviewed Kennedy for three hours and made him the first white person to appear on the cover of *Ebony*.

Ralph Waldo Emerson's must-read essay "Compensation" says, "There is a third silent party to all our bargains. The nature and soul of things takes on itself the guaranty of the fulfillment of every contract, so that honest service cannot come to loss. If you serve an ungrateful master, serve him the more. Put God in your debt. Every stroke shall be repaid. The longer the payment is withholden, the better for you; for compound interest on compound interest is the rate and usage of this exchequer."

This certainly held true for John Johnson. Shortly after Kennedy was elected, he invited him and his wife to dinner at the White House. They were going to dine with Thomas Watson, the president and founder of IBM. At dinner, Kennedy suddenly asked, "Mr. Watson, do you know if you do any advertising in any of John Johnson's magazines?"

Watson said, "I don't know. Do we, John?"

To which John Johnson responded, "No, as a matter of fact, my people have been knocking at your door, and none of your people are receptive or responsive."

Watson pulled out his personal diary and wrote in it, looked up at John, and said, "Tomorrow that changes."

Immediately, John Johnson began getting tens of millions of advertising dollars from IBM all because of one fortuitous dinner meeting. Johnson had created a brand-new marketplace.

As he relays this in his book, he says, "We must network and be available to eavesdrop in the right centers of influence."

Are you in the right centers of influence? If you're not, write in your future diary what centers of influence you want to be in, because if you're hanging out with the right people, you get the right results, and it becomes effortless effort. That's what networking is all about.

Everyone can learn to network step-by-step, no matter how humble, no matter how impoverished, no matter how backward, no matter how ignorant you may be to start with.

Start networking. It doesn't matter how you start. It matters that you start. It matters that you're going in the direction of becoming a great, grand, and terrific networker.

Write down a list of two hundred names of the people you want to meet, spend time with, grow with, play with, work with, earn money with, be more spiritual with, at depth. Write down all the questions that you want to ask. In my book *Dare to Win*, I listed the two hundred people that I wanted to meet, and I keep adding to that list. When you meet them, don't cross their names off. Instead, write down, "Victory" after their names and keep them in your address file along with the main facts about them. In his book *How to Swim with Sharks without Being Eaten Alive*, Harvey Mackay lists questions that he asks people. Keep track of the names of their kids, their spouses, their birthdays. If they have a company, buy a share of stock in it to stay updated.

Do you know what's happening? People reading my books finds out that they know a given person. They call me up and say, "I can get you to him or her. Let's have dinner." Or "I've got a meeting. They're going to be there. I'd like you to meet." All because I wrote down and shared the names. Have a list of must-meet names. Go for the easy ones first and get positive momentum, and it'll reinforce you to keep adding more names. It builds your self-esteem, because you'll be in the energy orbit of great people. You'll quickly discover that you have more resources, talents, interpersonal skills than you ever thought.

In Asia, when you sit with an Asian that is in the know, they lay out two sheets of paper. One lists their ten macro goals: what they want to accomplish during their lifetime. On one guy's list, he mentioned that he wanted to do an airline. I said, "Look, I've been on the board of the world's biggest airline; I'll introduce you to the chairman of the board." They started doing business.

The other page lists all the names of the people the person wants to meet, along with the person's curriculum vitae. Do the same thing: have a list of names of the who's who and who's through that you want to meet with. Oftentimes getting to the who's through is easy, and they're still well connected. They know everybody that's anybody, because they've been there and they've done that.

4. **Networking is fun, profitable, and enriching.** Once Jack Canfield and I were doing a seminar in Hawaii, and one morning we were playing out at the pool with our kids, family, and all the friends that we'd made in this seminar. All of a sudden, one of our classmates ran in with our dear friend and colleague, the late psychotherapist Dr. Wayne Dyer. Wayne was the best-selling author of many books, such as *Your Erroneous Zones*, *Change Your Thoughts, Change Your Life*, and *The Power of Intention*. He'd been a friend of mine for twenty-five years.

Wayne came along carrying his little tape recorder and sat down in a beach chair with Jack and me. Within a few minutes the whole pool emptied out and everyone came over to encircle us. Together with Wayne, we immediately started doing a spontaneous, applause-getting seminar. People started asking questions, and pretty soon the parents were sending their little kids up to their rooms to get cameras. They were getting pictures of Wayne, Jack, and Mark all at the poolside having a seminar together.

Again, networking—it's fun, profitable, and enriching the network. You learn a lot in those sessions. I always go back and take copious notes of what was said and what I thought.

I've got my list, which extends to thousands and thousands of people I want to play with, grow with, be expanded by, learn from, If you see it as fun, you'll go forward. If you see this as a tear-filled process and think, "I can't do that. I can't shake hands. I can't meet him or her; I'd be intimidated," you'll have difficulties, but if you think it's fun, it'll be fun.

The meaning in life comes out of the meaning that we put into life. There's no intrinsic meaning in your life, except that which you give it. You've got to put the meaning into life. Helen Keller was deaf and blind, but after her work with her teacher Annie Sullivan, she discovered that she could see with her inner eye better than most people could see with their external vision. She said, "If my candle is lit and yours isn't, light yours from mine. It doesn't take anything from mine, but it makes the world fourfold brighter."

That's the kind of networking I want you to do. I want you to be an insider at helping somebody that nobody else will help. When you help somebody who is unable to help you back, you are rewarded openly. The Bible says, "That thine alms may be in secret: and thy Father which seeth in secret himself shall reward thee openly" (Matthew 6:4).

If you give to get accolades and praise, you get paid once, but if you give in secret, you're rewarded forever.

Annie Sullivan became Helen Keller's Master Mind partner, taught her to think, and taught her to share. Helen became one of the most profound communicators of all time and networked with the famous figures of the world: everybody wanted to meet Helen Keller.

You can come from inauspicious beginnings, but if you think networking is fun, profitable, and enriching, you can meet everyone.

5. **Networking can be learned and taught.** I want you to watch a movie called *Stand and Deliver*, about the great Jaime Escalante. Jaime made his fortune in the computer business and then came back to the barrio of East LA. He decided that he could teach the principles of calculus to teenagers. He told his students, "If you don't learn calculus, you're going to be flipping hamburgers for your entire life."

One wise guy said, "Look, I flip hamburgers. See that TransAm out there with flames on it? That's my car. Mr. Escalante, I saw you walk here, so you must be a loser."

The kid didn't know that Jaime owned several Rolls-Royces and was financially free; he didn't throw that in their faces. Rather, he continued to sell them on the idea of being educated and self-educated. In fact, he had them dance calculus.

At first, when they took the SAT test, people from Boston swooped down and said, "You cheated."

Jaime said, "No. You're redlining us because we're Hispanic. We dance calculus step-by-step. We learned it, we mastered it, and we know how to take any test you want."

Jaime's students retook the test. They excelled the second time and gained entry into America's most prestigious schools on scholarships.

As I've been saying, let's get kinesthetic in our learning. Jean Houston teaches kinesthetically, and she has you dance everything that you learn. In the future, I hope to have a dance instructor help me teach some of the principles that I want you to learn.

Imagine networking like that in all our schools—if we had great, inspiring teachers to galvanize our spirits, stab our spirits alive, and make us want to learn something like calculus.

6. **Enroll others to become great networkers.** Trammell Crow, probably the world's biggest commercial builder, did a phenomenal job, starting with just a little bit of wealth and building warehouses down in Dallas when people needed him. He kept growing and glowing and showing. People came to him and said, "I want to do what you do."

Trammell Crow said, "OK, here's what we'll do."

Here's how hundreds of people have made millions of dollars. Trammell owns 100 percent of his main holding company. Then he allows 50/50 partnerships in subsidiaries of his master company. Those people put their in life energy, he puts his masterful thinking in, and he builds warehouse after warehouse around the country. It is a great way of getting networkers to work together in an omnieffective way.

Are you ready to meet terrific people like Trammell Crow and enroll them in working with you and sometimes for you?

7. **Networkers set goals to meet people on their networking list.** I wanted to meet Trammell Crow, so I met him. I want to meet Red Skelton, so I walked up to him and said, "Red, I've been a fan of yours for a long time."

"It's a hot day," he said. "I need a fan."

"Is it true that you've got a photographic memory?"

"Yeah, but it's underdeveloped."

As we talked for an hour and a half in a red-carpet room in LAX, I said to him, "I'm going to do a TV show."

"Look, Mark," he said, "do it the way Bob Hope and I do. Own the TV show; ask for the broadcast rights."

Later I found myself negotiating about the show, and I asked for the broadcast rights.

The man I was negotiating with asked, "Who told you to ask for that?"

To which I replied, "Red Skelton."

He thought for a fraction of a second and said, "You can have them."

That's why you're going to network with people who've done what you want to do.

8. **Networkers share their list of written goals and names with other like-minded networkers.**

One day I was in John Wayne Airport in Newport Beach, California, with my wife. It was totally shut down, and I needed to fly out. At the time, there was a nice little restaurant there run by a mom and pop, called Delaney's. As we went to eat, the head of the Federal Aviation Administration came in (she was dating my wife's first husband), so we all started chatting.

When I asked her why the airport was shut down, "Billy Graham's flying in, and they've got a threat on his life, so they've shut down the whole airport."

"I want to meet Dr. Graham," I said.

She assured me that security was very tight but that she would introduce me to the head of security. The guy said, "Look, buddy, your name is not on this list. There are only eleven people who can meet Dr. Graham at this airport."

I was determined to meet him, because he was on my list in my future diary. I saw him walk off the plane; he was deeply tanned, wearing a cap, and with a very pronounced gait. He was carrying a lot of newspapers under his arm, and nineteen armed security guards descended on him.

When Billy was almost alone, waiting for his baggage, I walked up to him, put up my hand, and said, "Billy, how are you?" knowing that he'd pressed flesh with millions of people.

Billy didn't have a clue to whether he knew me or not, but we spent a half hour talking and had a great time.

I said, "What are you here for?"

"To fill the Coliseum with a hundred thousand people a night. I've got to do ten to twelve radio and TV shows and some special shows at churches to make sure it's filled." Then he went on to say, "Mark, you talk to salespeople and networkers: tell them they've got to keep being masterful at prospecting. If this is true for me at age seventy plus, then it's true for any of them at whatever age."

9. **Get pictures of yourself with influential people.** Networkers have pictures taken of themselves with prominent political leaders, celebrities, empire builders, world servers, and the influential people of our time.

It's easy to do; just ask them. Today you're probably carrying a smartphone, which has a camera built in, so it's always at hand. Just say, "May I take a picture with you, please?" You'll be amazed at how many pictures you can collect.

The first time I saw a powerful photo wall library was when I went to visit Dr. Norman Vincent Peale's offices in Pawling, New York. It wowed me. Peale knew and had befriended everyone worth knowing. After that day, I made it my goal to do the same (and obviously that day I got a picture with Peale).

If you ever come to our office in Newport Beach, California and walk through our conference room, I think you'll be astounded at the people and faces that you'll recognize from around the world because I've gone out of my way to meet the who's who. I put these pictures in books, brochures, newsletters, on my website. Why? Because it gives credibility. You say, "Whoa! This person must be somebody, because they're standing there with Jay Leno or Dr. Robert Schuller or Billy Graham, or the president of the United States."

10. **Networkers stay actively in touch with the people on their lists.** Master marketers know that you've got to stay in touch with somebody at least seven times a year so that they don't forget you. Otherwise, you've got to make such a great impression that you're totally memorable and unforgettable. Stay in touch with people by phone, letter, fax, audio, videotape, email, or whatever means it takes.

Master marketers send out information on a regular basis. They have an A list, whom they invite to the parties and to whom they send out pictures of the family. If you send out cards, letters, thank-yous, memos, tapes, notes, emails, or articles that are of interest to your friends multiple times a year, you're building friendship and networking equity.

Friendship and networking equity can cause your rapid ascent in business and in life, because if they don't remember you, they can't refer you, recommend you, or give you business. In his book *New Rules for the New Economy*, Kevin Kelly says, "We're cloaking the globe with a networked society."

11. Master networkers create functions and events. One of the greatest networking function mavens was publisher Malcolm Forbes. Just look at the parties he had. It cost him $2 million to get the who's who to his house in Tangier, but the next month, he did a billion dollars' worth of business in advertising revenues for his *Forbes* magazine.

Malcolm owned a yacht called *The Capitalist Tool*. It was extravagant. It had everything—a helicopter, a racing boat, movie theater, and all the toys and amenities. Malcolm hosted every living president on his yacht and engraved the cup they had used to keep as a memento.

Probably you don't own a yacht. Here's where you start. I've asked beginning chiropractors to sponsor a free breakfast monthly and have all their clients, patients, and customers bring a friend whom they can meet over food. It works. Don't flip flapjacks that day. Your job is to press flush, smile, glad-hand, meet people. Start the events where you are, start them small, and make them tall.

12. **Networking is a skill.** Most of the people I've met with have superior skills that they've chosen to master. They have chosen to model individuals with superior networking skills. Recent presidential role models with superb people skills include Ronald Reagan, George H. W. Bush, and Bill and Hillary Clinton.

Each builds rapport, is charismatic, smiles, has a genuine, authentic handshake, embraces you with their spirit, and makes you feel instantly comfortable and at ease.

These people also ask about you quickly and listen deeply. You've really got to listen to what people are saying to you, then respond and be ready to go to work. Great professionals in every field master the fine art of networking.

Learn the network. Watch the masters. Take all the trainings you can in networking. Observe all the greats, like Lee Iacocca, former head of the Chrysler Corporation. He personally went through all their trainings. He practically made it mandatory for his staff to take the Dale Carnegie course or join Toastmasters International or the National Speakers Association.

When you associate with the best people, their goodness rubs off and it rubs in. Soon you'll become a master networker. Jeannette Vos, author of *The Learning Revolution*, said, "The more you link, the more you learn."

Your networking goal is to have a huge and growing number of friends. Keep meeting new friends. Keep the old friends; figure out who your true friends are, the ones that are going to stand with you shoulder to shoulder and back-to-back when you're under attack.

Be forever expanding and increasing your list of contacts. It's an asset of immeasurable and unconquerable value. Be a fearless networker. Build your list with names of quality people that you care about, that you want to serve and be served by. In the beginning, it might be a slight struggle to get this process down, but there are many people who can help you meet everyone you want to meet. Be on the lookout for an enthusiastic super networker; they exist; buddy up to them.

Ask who are the supernetworkers in your group, association, or industry. Because they're master networkers, they'll meet you, impress you, and even ask how they can serve you. Tell them whom you want to meet. If you know exactly whom you want to meet, state their name; you'll probably be whisked into the presence of that person immediately.

Remember, there are plenty of people willing and wanting to help. Their humble request is that someday, somewhere, you pass on the favor to someone else.

If you've got something that you want to accomplish, go through the magazines in your industry, association, or business, the newspapers, or the main magazines of the world. Remember, the better your network, the higher your network.

10

Go and Grow

In this chapter, I'll give you several real-life examples of people who have achieved greatness against all odds. They will inspire you to achieve your own greatness. They illustrate the truth stated by Napoleon Hill: "Whatever the mind of man can conceive and believe, it can achieve."

Black Diamonds

Let's start with the great black leader Booker T. Washington. Booker T. Washington was born in 1856 and was raised by his mother. At that time in Malden, West Virginia, no blacks were literate. A young black from Ohio was kind enough to teach little Booker how to read using the Webster speller, which was the number one book of its time. Booker read it so much that grownups started calling him "Booker."

Kids tormented him with his nickname. When he went to school, the teacher asked him, "What's your name?"

He said, "Booker."

"Booker what?"

"Booker Washington," he said, because *Washington*, as far as he was concerned, was the proudest name in history.

His answer stuck. Later, Andrew Carnegie said, "History will tell us of two Washingtons—one white and one black, both fathers of their people."

After much difficulty, Booker got to Hampton Institute in Virginia Beach, Virginia, for his education in 1872. To fast-forward the story, Booker founded Tuskegee Institute, America's first black vocational school cum university, in Alabama.

Washington was big. He believed big and achieved big. He achieved what most people thought impossible: that blacks could have their own school and learn and get advanced degrees. Booker made a commitment to God that he would educate his people. His aim was to make small men and women great: he wanted everyone to bud, flower, and fruit, he said. He also said, "I found that success is measured not by the position attained in life, as by the obstacles with which you have to overcome in attaining that position."

When Booker was a sophomore, he heard the phrase *noblesse oblige*. To him, it meant those who get superior advantages of schooling are morally obliged to pass that opportunity on to those less fortunate than themselves. He said he had a subconscious desire to teach and to share. He caught and taught the poet's phrase: "Our echoes roll from soul to soul." He learned, and he shared. Learn more, earn more, and share more.

When I visited the museum in Tuskegee, I saw a book there called *Black Diamonds*, a collection of quotations from Booker T. Washington. They apply as much today as they did back when he wrote them. I'd ask you to read it, savor it, and drink it in deeply.

The Wizard from Tuskegee

A contemporary of Booker T. Washington, George Washington Carver, became one of America's greatest scientists, educators, and inventors. Born in 1864, at the end of slavery, George was a sickly kid, who looked like a brown baby bird, all head and eye. He had a high voice and stuttered when he talked. He loved all living things. He loved the woods and studied everything in nature. He loved reading the Bible that his aunt Marielle had given him. He also taught himself to play the accordion so he'd never be lonely.

After slavery ended, it was difficult for a black person to get into any school, but George got into school at age twelve. He learned fast. He went through each year

of school in half the time it took other students because
he was hungry to know and to learn, and he desperately
wanted to help his people.

A teacher, Miss Etta Bud, helped George get into agricultural school at Iowa State College at age thirty. He
achieved extraordinary success. He avidly studied geol-
ogy, botany, chemistry, and zoology. The more George
learned, the more he wanted everyone else to learn, especially Southern black farmers, who were depleting their
soil by overgrowing cotton and tobacco on their land.
George thought, "If I could teach farmers how to make
better farms, I'll be doing something good for people."

George was not yet famous, but attracted the attention of Booker T. Washington at Tuskegee. Mr. Washington wanted George to come and teach at Tuskegee in a
new department of agriculture. George wanted to teach
young black farmers about soil, plants, and farming.
George wrote to Booker T. and said, "It has always been
one of the great ideas of my life to be of the greatest good
to the greatest number of my people, and to this end, I've
been preparing myself for these many years. I feel that
this line of education is the key to unlock the golden door
of freedom to our people."

When George arrived at Tuskegee Normal School
(as it was then called), he found only one brick building.
It was not like Iowa State, with beautiful buildings and
lawns. Here there was nothing but acres and acres of dirt.

Booker T. raised the money to buy the materials. The agricultural building would be designed by George and built brick by brick by the students. Dr. Carver started with thirteen complaining students, who didn't have a laboratory or tools with which to work.

"There's no time to whine, 'Oh, if only I had so and so or such and such,'" Dr. Carver said, "Do it anyhow. Use what you find around you." Students found old bottles, jars, boxes, pieces of string, tin, rubber, and wires; they searched garbage cans and dumps to build the homemade laboratory.

Dr. Carver had nothing but uncommon ambition and a purpose bigger than he was, and he turned these qualities into something great. He set up a farm on school grounds, with experimental plots on twenty acres. He improved poor soil in two ways: he put nitrogen fertilizer into it, and he grew plants like sweet potatoes and peanuts, which would add nitrogen to the soil. He taught the students to create compost of cut grass, leaves, manure, cover it with rich soil from the woods or swamps, and make exhausted soil rich again. He then planted legumes such as peas, beans, and peanuts. Legumes, which grow in pods, take nitrogen from the air and release it through the roots as they grow, enriching the soil. He also developed systems of crop rotation, which freed the South from growing tobacco and cotton only.

Dr. Carver became the most popular teacher at Tuskegee. He wanted his students to know every plant and insect. To play a joke on him, the students caught an ant, a beetle, a spider, and a moth. They cut them up, glued the parts together to make a funny-looking insect, and handed it to Dr. Carver, asking, "What is it?"

"Well," he said, "I think it is what you call humbug."

Dr. Carver wanted every farmer to plant a sweet potato patch. Sweet potatoes are easy to grow, and they replenish the soil with nitrogen. The next year, the farmers could plant cotton again and have the best crop ever. The trouble was, there was no market for all the sweet potatoes that they grew.

Dr. Carver went into his laboratory and locked the doors. He discovered that sweet potatoes could be made into flour, starch, sugar, molasses, vinegar, ink, dye, and glue. He developed over a hundred products and created a brand-new market for his people.

In 1914, the cotton crop was devastated by boll weevils. Dr. Carver began experiments with peanut in order to promote them as a replacement for the lost cotton crop.

At this point, farmers were willing to listen. Dr. Carver discovered 105 different foods that could be made with peanuts, and made over three hundred brand-new products, including peanut butter. Carver once made an entire meal with peanuts: soup, mock cheese, milk, buttermilk, mock chicken, cream, vegetable salad, cookies, ice cream, and coffee. None of his guests knew that the foods were all made with peanuts until he told them.

Dr. Carver also created washing powder, bleach, shoe polish, metal polish, ink, rubbing oil, cooking oil, axle grease, cattle feed, thirty different dyes, plastic, shampoo, soap, and shaving cream from peanuts; he even made linoleum and rubber from the shells. He was so intent on showing his discoveries to desperate farmers that he created a Tuskegee school on wheels.

Dr. Carver's best students shared his new insights, which gave farmers hope, profits, and a future. In Dr. Carver's view, God had given him these discoveries, and now he had the privilege of bestowing them on others.

As a result, Tuskegee grew to 156 teachers, 83 buildings, and 1,500 students by 1906. Dr. Carver was called "the wizard from Tuskegee." He could have gotten rich by patenting his breakthrough discoveries, but he gave his ideas to his people for their advancement. In fact, he donated his life savings to continue research on behalf of humankind. He said, "What is money when I have all the earth?"

Dr. Carver turned down working with the world's greatest inventor, Thomas Alva Edison, saying, "If I were to go with you, Mr. Edison, my work would not be known as mine, and my people would not get the credit. I want my people to have the credit for whatever I do."

Dr. Carver found acres of diamonds in his mind at Tuskegee in rotating crops with sweet potatoes and peanuts. Answers come to those who faithfully ask and keep moving forward, confidently and courageously, with whatever resources they have.

Goethe said, "Boldness has power in it." Carver wanted his people, who had just come out of slavery, to have opportunities to make their farms grow cash crops beyond cotton. Thanks to his inventive, imaginative mind, he was able to benefit everyone.

Everyone has an imagination. Each of us can invent new and profitable solutions for ourselves and others. It only takes one great invention to enrich you, your family, and our entire world.

Working inventively, Dr. Carver gained respect, love, admiration, and appreciation. He chose to be unstoppable, and so can you. Carver didn't let race, lack of schools, lack of supplies, or apparent lack of opportunities slow him down, and you shouldn't either. No one can stop you unless you let them.

If you're facing an overwhelming problem, choose to turn it inside out and find the hidden benefit. Napoleon Hill said, "Every adversity has a seed of equivalent or greater benefit in it." Problems are assets if you reconceive them as Carver did.

Carver lived to help others and to do the best he could. Each of us is asked, and I hope, inspired, to do the same. Infinite growth is possible for each of us if we have a vision and keep expanding and sharing it with like-minded others. We need to awaken the Booker T. Washington and George Washington Carver in each and every one of us. They made something great out of nothing, and we can too.

A Hundred Whaling Walls

The next person I want to talk to you about is a great friend of mine named Robert Wyland. Since elementary school, Wyland had been told that he had great artistic ability. Wyland would paint and draw around the clock. When his aunt took him to the beach, he saw a breaching whale. He instantly started painting whales, but at first he couldn't give his artwork away. Nonetheless, he kept working constantly until he found his market.

Wyland opened his first gallery in Laguna Beach, California, and he painted the side of the building with his first Whaling Wall, and it's a showstopper. If you're driving down the Pacific Coast Highway, you can't help but see it and say, "Whoa." Many people stop their car, turn around, park, and just gaze at it; then they go into his gallery. He now has forty galleries around the world.

Wyland's mission is to inspire a whole generation of people to become more aware of and involved with our oceans and the life within them. His goal is to promote and protect our precious ocean resources through his Wyland Foundation. To keep expanding his market, he has now painted a hundred Whaling Walls around America.

Some of you remember the great movie from 1993 called *Free Willy*. Wyland went down to Mexico and painted a Whaling Wall, sold it for $2 million, used all the money to take Keiko, the whale that played Willy in the film, from Mexico up to Oregon. There he painted another wall to raise enough money to keep that animal alive until he could be freed. He's a great man with a great spirit and a great heart.

Wyland is the greatest master of ocean imagery on the planet. He helps us discover the undersea mysteries of whales, dolphins, turtles, and other fantastic marine life. He is convinced that he's on a mission to save the planet, and I appreciate him as a crusader.

My family and I stayed at Wyland's house in Hawaii for several days, and I watched this master paint. When he starts a painting, it's like when I start writing: it's scratchy, it's gawky, it's ordinary. But after just a few seconds, you become absorbed by this process. He usually starts with the eye, because the eyes are the portals to the soul. He says, "If you look in the eye of a whale once, it will change you forever." He's a master's master.

In 2003, Wyland, Jack Canfield, and I collaborated on *Chicken Soup for the Ocean Lovers' Soul: Amazing Sea Stories and Wyland Artwork to Open the Heart and Rekindle the Spirit*.

Wyland started with nothing but his love for the ocean and a whale that he saw. He is a visionary leader. He has made himself into one of the best known, best loved, most creative people on the planet, and has created something great and organic that will keep growing forever. His dream as a planetary citizen is to save the oceans quickly. The goal of this book is to help you take your ordinary idea and make it extraordinary, and when it's extraordinary, guess what? You'll become extraordinary. I can feel your heart opening to that idea.

"I Am Somebody"

I want to talk about a guy named Howard Schultz, the founder of Starbucks. For hundreds of years, people have been drinking coffee. Who would ever have believed that someone could come up with an idea that would make coffee bars work and turn them into major meeting places?

Howard got started locally, in Seattle, with just one Starbucks, but he told everybody that he was going to be bigger than McDonald's. His goal was to open up one Starbucks every day around the world, and now he's done it and is doing it.

So why not think big? Network big. Build your dreams, and then go out and let them grow.

The example of Andrew Carnegie taught me that ordinary people might even have an advantage over privileged people when it comes to thinking big and achieving greatness. You may not have famous relatives or friends in high places. You may be a common laborer working at minimum wage. It doesn't matter. What's going to launch you into quantum growth is your decision to be somebody.

The black leader Jesse Jackson always tells kids in school, "I am somebody." Then he asks them to jab themselves in the chest and say it. If you've never done that, you need to, because the central message of this chapter is that anyone can become somebody special, somebody with influence, somebody with power, somebody with wealth, as long as you've got a goal.

If you don't have a goal, your goal is to set some goals. You can be somebody who makes a difference, somebody who has mastered the art of thinking big, and then you can achieve your goals and inspire others to achieve theirs.

Do you want to live at a prestigious address? Own several homes? Drive a luxury automobile worth over $100,000? These are the results of thinking big and taking systematic steps to achieve your goals. So what if no one famous ever came from your city? You can become that first famous person.

What about the fact that your education is limited? You can become self-educated. As Jim Rohn says, "Your education begins when what we call your education is over." *Commencement* means *to start*, and the end is the beginning. It doesn't matter whether you have a lot of academic degrees or none. All that matters is your degree of commitment. If you choose to educate yourself consistently one hour a day, in less than five years you'll be one of the all-time experts in your field of study. It doesn't matter if you have a special merit award, achievements, trophies, or medals. If you do well enough, you'll get lots of honorary degrees and doctorates; you're going to get applauded, you're going to get the awards, and you're going to get to travel.

Most people live and die untraveled. If you want to visit every exciting, glamorous place, you can go from where you are to where you intend to be. You can go to all the glistening, glorious houses and all the impressive places and palaces and see all the spectacular cities of the world. Often you'll see lonely, hurting, sick, troubled hearts. As your heart becomes untroubled, untangled, and forward-moving, you can help bring up all the other people around you. You can have an influence immediately on 250 people, and it can grow to any number you choose.

As you become successful, many people will say, "I launched you." I smile and let the people take all the credit, and I get all the results. One of the world's great insurance salesmen, Joe Gandolfo, said, "God, I'll give you all the credit; you give me all the commissions." Many people did help you.

Your decision today to become a big thinker is going to have you befriend the little people, the big people, and all the people in between. You're going to end up with connections with VIPs and the people with distinguished letters after their name. You're going to go from no list to the A list. You're going to have peers and friends who are professors, famous authors, powerful politicians, doctors, generals, lordly churchmen, kings, queens, and the rest of the leaders of the world.

You might say, "But wait a second, Mark. I don't have any organization." Well, the apostles of Jesus started out with no organization. They had rough, broken hands and broken speech. You can start out unpolished, uncultured, unlettered, and ignorant, and you can still suck it in, tough it out, and end up with an attitude of gratitude. You can take yourself and everybody around you to the absolute top.

Why would you want to die in poverty when you can leave a continuing legacy? You can have your own home, your own insurance, a retirement plan that will beat the band, and earn financial freedom. You can raise money to pay taxes for you and all of your friends. Jesus did that when he told Peter to fish and find a coin in the fish's mouth: "Go thou to the sea, and cast an hook, and take up the fish that first cometh up; and when thou hast opened his mouth, thou shalt find a piece of money: that take, and give unto them for me and thee" (Matthew 17:27).

What does this mean? If you've got taxes to pay, pay them, and remember to pay your tithes so you stay open and free and under the spot where all the good things pour out.

Leave a legacy like Andrew Carnegie's three thousand libraries and his vision for world peace. In 1910, he founded the Carnegie Endowment for International Peace. In 1914, World War I was about to break out. No one knew it was going to be a world war, but Carnegie had an idea that this would be the greatest war of all time. He got an audience with Kaiser Wilhelm II of Germany. He sat down with him, signed his name to a check, gently pushed it across the table, and said, "If you will stay out of war, you can fill this check out for any amount you want and have it."

Kaiser Wilhelm ripped up the check, threw it in Carnegie's face, and told him to get out of there. Although Carnegie was living in his Scottish castle at the time, he knew what was going to happen, so he quickly gathered his family and went back to Pittsburgh, where he lived until the war was over.

Andrew Carnegie is a great inspiration to me. He did great thinking not only with his gift of libraries, and his desire for peace, but by building New York's Carnegie Hall, which hosts great concerts. If you're in New York City, you can take a tour of his house. You'll see that he had affirmations that inspired him to take action carved in the walls.

For Better and Better

If you're single, thinking big is going to help you get married. For thirty-one years, I was single. I had written down that my ideal wife would be an intellectual voluptuary with great self-discipline. As Cavett Robert once told me, I way outmarried myself. Although it's totally true, my wife and I are a perfect balancing act for each other.

If you're in a marriage, you can have all the friendship, encouragement, and companionship of a spouse (and children, if you want them), and it'll be among the greatest treasures of your life.

My wife and I get remarried every year, and we write our own marital vows. The first time I did that, I wrote, "We got married for better and better." If you get what you affirm, why would you want to marry for better or worse?

Zig Ziglar said he was flying across the country and saw this old boy who had his wedding band on his index finger. Zig said, "Excuse me, sir, but aren't you wearing your wedding band on the wrong finger?"

"Married the wrong woman," the man said. He never thought about being the right guy.

In our vows, we say that we got married for healthy and healthier. This doesn't mean that I'm not going to have a health challenge; it just means we're going to handle it.

One Saturday night years ago, Patty and I were asleep, and our daughter came in, nudged us, and said, "Mommy, Daddy, would it be bad if you sniffed a pussy willow into your nose?" My wife is such a deep sleeper that it's tough to wake her up, but she bounced up in bed and said, "You did what?"

"I sucked it into my nose," my daughter said. She pointed above her left eyebrow and said, "It's right here now, Mommy, and it really hurts."

We went to an urgent care center. By now it was the middle of the night, and the doctor could not figure out how to get the pussy willow out without cutting her open.

"That just doesn't do," I said. "Look, I did a set of tapes called *Visualizing Is Realizing*, and let me give it to you quickly. Go into a closed-eye trance, and tilt your inner eyes up at a forty-five-degree angle. If I had sixty-beat music like Pachelbel's *Canon in D*, I'd play it, but just run that rhythm through your head and say, 'I know the solution, I know the solution, I know the solution,' and you and I are going to agree that you're going to have it in thirty seconds."

The doctor's eyes popped open and bugged out as if he had a thyroid condition. He said, "I golf with a pediatric eye, ear, nose, and throat guy." Although it was 2:30 a.m. on a Sunday morning, he called his friend up, and the friend said, "Just have the Hansens at my office at eight tomorrow morning."

We went in, and in a nanosecond, the doctor got the pussy willow out painlessly and effortlessly.

When we affirm that we're going to have health, we're not saying that we're never going to have some conditions or circumstances show up. It just means that we're going to figure out how to handle them.

Why not write your affirmations for what you want—for more and more love, for more and more intimacy, for 125 years, with options for renewal?

You can have it all, and you can have it fast. Five years from now, you can have a growing empire that is spawning other empires. The whole world is overflowing and ever flowing with opportunity. You can become the person you want to be. You can have a life that is extraordinary and beautiful. You can be the solution rather than the problem. You can turn on the light and cast out the darkness. You can make your fear disappear and do that for others too. Consider this: if you normally only use 10 percent of your mind powers when you started reading this book and your ideas double to 20 percent of your mind power, that's a 100 percent increase. Wow. If, for the sake of argument, you're earning $100,000, you'll now earn $200,000. The law of increase says, "To him who increases, more will be added." Note also that addition will happen without ceasing if you believe it'll happen without ceasing.

Look at Ted Turner. He owns one percent of the land in America. He's called Captain Outrageous. He took over his father's little signage company and made it work. Then he went to NBC and tried to sell his concept of "all the news while it's happening." They told him to get out. He said, "That's OK. I'm going to start CNN." Then he decided to become the philanthropists of philanthropists, to be the first one ever to give $1 billion.

I love Captain Outrageous, and I'm asking you to be outrageous in your life at levels you didn't even think you could be outrageous at, because the purpose of life is to grow. Grow yourself, grow spiritually, grow mentally, grow physically, grow your business and grow your future.

11

The End Is a Beginning

Every end is a new beginning. Most of us have to have a real paradigm shift to see endings and beginnings in this way. But if you can, a whole new world of possibilities and accomplishments will be open to you.

Everyone knows the ironclad law of cause and effect. The effect can never be greater than the cause: sow, and you shall reap. The thought and the thing are one. Cause and effect are one. The acorn is going to become an oak tree. It can't become a kumquat or a tomato.

This is called the law of identification: the thing has to become itself. If you think billion-dollar thoughts, you get billion-dollar results. A good student becomes a graduate. A bad student stumbles through and may not graduate. A young, hard-charging businessman evolves into a tycoon or empire builder.

I do a lot of graduation ceremonies, and I say, "Every end is a new beginning. The tassel is worth the hassle." As I've said, when you end school, you're beginning your real education, which is a self-education. It's a brand-new beginning.

Wisdom from the Dalai Lama

I had the privilege of learning from His Holiness the Dalai Lama at a talk in Pasadena a number of years ago. He is, of course, the spiritual leader of millions of Tibetan Buddhists, many of whom have been exiled by the Chinese communist government. He is a blissful, kind, deep, prolific writer and a scientifically aware human being. When he came onstage before twenty thousand people, my eyes spontaneously watered, and I felt my heart chakra open and expand in his presence.

His Holiness's first line was, "I'm just a simple Buddhist monk, here to promote human values, understanding, and ethics for the new millennium." He went on to say, "Infinite altruism exists only in human beings and the animal kingdom."

What a concept! That's what America has been doing for a long time. After they make a lot of money, most people become philanthropists. John Wesley, the wealthy English minister who started the Methodist movement, had a classic line: "Earn all you can, save all you can, invest all you can, and then give all you can."

Giving all you can is altruism. You don't always have to give with money. You can give a smile, a pat on the back, encouragement, a letter, a note, an endorsement, or a recommendation. The Dalai Lama is saying that you and I have the ability to be infinitely altruistic. If you're altruistic for good reasons and you have no ulterior end in mind, the bigger world, God, and infinite intelligence have a brand-new end that is going to ripple back toward you.

It's like skipping a stone in a lake: the stone goes out into the lake, and but its wave starts to propagate: the wave is multiplied, magnetized, and magnified. When you put out infinite altruism in the universe, you may be doing it with no end in sight, but greater and grander good is going to come your way.

The Dalai Lama went on to say that eliminating fear is good for the heart and the health. He said we must see our problems from different angles, widening our minds and perspectives and involving ourselves in analytical meditation.

When you're looking at a problem from only one direction, you say, "I'm out of work." You start to feel downtrodden, despondent, and disconsolate and you shut down. Why not look at the situation this way?

"Holy cow, I got fired. This is the greatest thing ever. I've got 360 degrees of possibility. There are 37,000 occupations. I can now do what I've always wanted to do." See it from all angles.

I'm going to plant the seed in you, but different seeds bring forth plants of different colors. How do you want to color your future as you end your seed life and enter your plant life, where you're going to bud and flower?

The Dalai Lama said we all share the values of love, compassion, tolerance, and forgiveness, whether we call our ultimate destination heaven, nirvana, or by some other name. Wouldn't it be nice to be a little more ecumenical?

Some years ago, I won an award that tested my self-worthiness: the Council of Churches and Synagogues voted me the humanitarian of the year. I didn't feel entirely worthy of this great award, which has been given to Nelson Mandela and other giants. In any case, this organization tries to create tolerance by encouraging people go to a different church, synagogue, or temple at least once a year in order to broaden their perspectives. Those who do this grow and become more spiritually aware. I've learned that the people at the top in religion don't fight very much. It's the people at the bottom that try to beat each other up.

His Holiness went on to say that religious diversity serves humanity; each religion is unique and enriches all others. "We need a different context," he said, "one that recognizes that we can all discuss the differences but are aware of the multitude of similarities."

In 1999, the Dalai Lama assembled the fifteen greatest, wisest spiritual leaders representing the five largest religions—major players, like Bishop Desmond Tutu. They all agreed to speak with one voice about global concerns that they could agree on. They want humanity to mature, to be on a sound ground, and move to a healthier, less violent world. They want to ban nuclear weapons and inhumane acts against other human beings. Nonviolence is more than just an alternative; it's a necessity in a world where nuclear war is capable of annihilating virtually 100 percent of humanity.

Our only choice, according to His Holiness, is dialogue. We need to have communication. We need to connect. We need to talk to one another. The Dalai Lama is a big and courageous thinker. He wants freedom, love, health, happiness, peace, and prosperity for everyone. He's not naive. He sees the world's spiritual crisis not as a reason to throw up our hands and give up, but as a new opportunity to come together in dialogue.

Our Nation's Self-Help Treasures

America is the greatest country in the world partly because we have self-help books, audios, videos and websites. Books like *Think and Grow Rich* by Napoleon Hill helped this country get out of the Depression in the 1930s.

No other country or continent has self-help products like ours. They don't come out of Asia, Africa, or Russia. You don't find a Dale Carnegie or a Wayne Dyer there. Nowhere else has an Og Mandino, Wallace D. Wattles, Bob Proctor, Ken Dychtwald, or Napoleon Hill. This unique gift has cultivated our nation's greatness, and its most important asset is human imagination.

Tom Peters, author of the must-read *Circle of Innovation*, says, "There is no excuse for not being great." We're blessed that the best learned how to do it and were generous enough to compress their life experience into biographies and autobiographies. If you read one of these, you'll get all that compressed learning. These sources can be immeasurably helpful to your future success.

I want to encourage you to read a thousand books in a decade. That's a hundred per year, two per week. I ask you to read one self-help action book and one biography or autobiography per week. It will, I promise, awaken your destiny.

My friend, the Australian Peter J. Daniels, is one of the world's richest men as well as a compelling speaker. He has personally read and analyzed over fifteen hundred biographies and autobiographies. The main question he asked is, "What makes the great, great?" His answer: a sense of destiny. He suggests—and I agree—that everyone has a sense of destiny, although it's usually buried by societal amnesia and the details of life.

Reading what others have done and are doing reawakens your higher self, your spiritual self, to your fullest potential. As you awaken, everyone around you starts to awaken as well. It's exciting to the max.

Another friend of mine, Jim Trelease, author of *The Reading-Aloud Handbook*, helps children to make books into friends. Jim teaches that we can turn on the turned off readers. We can show them that reading is fun and pleasant. Literature raises the HQ, the heart quotient, as well as the IQ. Jim teaches how childhood readers become lifetime readers, and he gives samples of the great books for reading aloud. He's a treat to experience, and I hope you'll take advantage of his work.

A Means to an End

Be aware that money is not an end in itself but a means to an end. Jim Rohn says, "I became a millionaire not for the millions, but for what you become in the process." He adds that envisioning the end is the beginning of realizing your dream. When presidential aspirants start their campaigns, they begin at the end. They visualize themselves at the inauguration, giving the address, and accepting congratulations for having won the contest for the world's most powerful office. They envision being in the Oval office. They think backwards and imagine what they need to do to accomplish this daunting task. They probably first dreamed of becoming president as children. Then in adulthood, they put themselves on an accelerated learning curve to become all they could possibly be in preparation for this high office. They had to comprehensively study politics, economics, law, language, world government, and world affairs. They had to master persuasion, thinking, and people skills. They needed to be able to handle day-to-day activities so effortlessly that they could apply their intelligence to creating the future. These aspirants studied the lives, successes, and failures of past presidents in order to gauge their own proper roles as president.

I want you think a little bit like a president. Let me take you inside a presidential office for a second, because I'm close friends with Doug Wead, who has been a special consultant to George Bush Sr. Doug says that every day the president gets a red file when he's eating his fruit at breakfast, and he's got to go over the most important decisions of the day. During a typical day in the president's life, he has eighty different meetings. Most people are really prepared when they go to see the president. They think they're going to get a lot of time, but in fact he only spends two or three minutes with each one before he is whisked from office to office.

If you want to maximize your time effectiveness, I'm asking you to think like a president. Have somebody that runs your state of affairs, a chief information officer, and somebody that delegates to make sure that you're doing the most efficient and effective thing at any given time.

Success on Two Hours a Day

Dr. Jeffrey Lant is a prolific writer and perhaps the highest paid self-help action writer of all times, and he's totally self-published. Here's a man who know how to see the end from the beginning.

Jeffrey graduated Phi Beta Kappa in English literature from Harvard. He wanted to think his way rich and created a ten-year storyboard on his working wall to inspire, motivate, and remind himself of where he's going. Could you do the same? Absolutely. If you haven't got a ten-year storyboard plan, why don't you?

Jeffrey began his writing career by deciding on the direction he would take and how much daily time he would invest in his writing each day. He knew that the British novelist Graham Greene wrote for only two hours a day and became immensely successful, so Jeffrey decided to write two hours every day, no matter what.

In two hours, Jeffrey writes a five-page, content-rich article that he sells three ways. First, as a special report for $6. He keeps the code in his computer and only prints it out when the customer's money has been processed. The computer printout costs 4 to 11 cents, so his return on investment is huge. Second, that special report is used as an article and sent to small circulation magazines. There are over 14,000 small circulation magazines in America, and their editors have trouble getting quality articles. They cheerfully publish Lant's insightful and refreshingly readable articles. That way, Jeffrey gets exposure to over 1.5 million readers per month. He only requests that he can briefly advertise his other writings. At the bottom of the article it says, "For 138 surefire get-ahead articles, call, write, or email Dr. Jeffrey Lant in Cambridge, Massachusetts." His exposure has grown by magazine by magazine, slowly but surely.

Every January 2, Jeffrey starts writing a new 600-page book which he finishes by July 2, which he sells for $40 per copy. He has over a million people in his database, and he knows that he is going to sell 25,000 books at $40. That's $1 million in his mailbox for a book he started on January 2 and finished on July 2. Then he goes on to Europe to buy Old Masters.

In his little workshop, Jeffrey has seven computers, which are always working on different projects. He has figured out how to write a special report, which becomes an article, which in turn becomes a mini-chapter in a book. He's getting paid three ways for the same piece of work, which takes only two hours a day, and nets millions more than any other writer. That's good thinking.

Jeffrey started at the end: where he wanted to be. He wanted to be a great writer, a great thinker, and a great author, but he also wanted to be a connoisseur of the finest pieces of artwork in the world. To do that, he had to give himself the challenge of making massive amounts of money in a very short time. I give his model to you because it's so replicable. I've used aspects of it myself.

Your Ten-Year Storyboard

Let's look at Jeffrey's philosophy to see what you can get from it now. Number one, Jeffrey has a ten-year plan. The end of the decade is his beginning. Try to create a ten-year plan. It will stretch your mind. Where do you want to be in a decade? What do you want to be doing? With whom? How much money do you want to be earning? How big and profitable is your database going to become?

Number two, as you keep studying and editing your ten-year picture storyboard, ideas will constantly flash into your mind. Once you have a big idea, you'll have little ideas, which will keep coming spontaneously to you, telling you how to accomplish your big idea. Remember them. Record them. Make them bigger than life.

Third, share your dream. Show it to like-minded, encouraging, enthusiastic people. Each time you tell your story, you'll have new interest and new ideas. Jot them down to enable your vision to evolve and grow organically.

Fourth, create a cookie-cutter formula, work it once, and get paid for it over and over. That will not only work in writing but in franchises, in licensing, in a lot of places. Ponder this idea deeply and profoundly.

Fifth, decide on your boundaries. Jeffrey writes two hours a day, but he's thinking perpetually. His desire to compile and share important money-making ideas is unstoppable, and for him it's great fun. Why not decide that whatever you're going to do is going to be fun? Why not make a life that is ecstasy for you? You'll look back on it and say, "I created a masterpiece."

Templeton's Laws of Life

The late Sir John Templeton was another big thinker who saw the end from the beginning. He was regarded on Wall Street as one of the world's wisest investors. He founded the hugely successful Templeton family of mutual funds. He started with a borrowed $10,000 and ended up with a multibillion-dollar fortune.

Sir John believed in the laws of life, holding that the common denominator of successful people and enterprise is the devotion to ethical and spiritual principles. These laws are truthfulness, perseverance, thrift, enthusiasm, humility, and altruism, which each of us can discover and develop. Sir John believed these will give you lasting friendships and significant financial rewards. He was also founder of the Templeton Progress in Religion Prize, whose past recipients included Mother Teresa, Billy Graham, the Dalai Lama. It espouses the goal of finding new ways to increase love and understanding of God.

In the early 1950s, John Templeton helped found the Young Presidents' Organization (YPO), a worldwide club headquartered in New York City, with approximately 29,000 members in more than 130 countries as of 2018. To be a YPOer, a person must have become, before age forty-five, the president or chairman and chief executive officer of a corporation of significance with a minimum revenue and minimum number of employees. Members have a wide range of socioeconomic, educational and cultural backgrounds. They receive an extraordinary education from the best presenters in the world and a worldwide network of influential and important friends. They do business with one another, help each other solve problems, and get the red-carpet treatment when they travel. John said that the similarity among these men and women is their perseverance. They don't give up.

You may be saying, "How does that affect me?" You could do the same thing or even better. All I'm trying to do is trigger your thinking in new, innovative ways. It's well worth it to think big today.

We're at the beginning of growth in America and in the world today, thanks to the Internet, computerization, communication, a learning revolution, and globalization.

Everybody is going to do business with everybody, and we're going to get there and we're going to get there fast.

Change is about reorganizing, reengineering, reinventing, reconceiving. When you reconceive a thought, a situation, a corporation, a product, you create a whole new order. Do that, and the creativity will flow. Change can be exhilarating, joyous, and liberating, but it can also be terrifying because you're questioning your own identity and sense of value. But take the risk; it's worth it.

My Hundred-Year Plan

Here's my hundred-year plan, my vision for 2100 AD. (By the way, let me respectfully ask you to send me a copy of yours if you write one. I'd like to put together a book of hundred-year plans from around the world.)

My first goal for a hundred years: feed unfed humanity expeditiously and considerately. As I mentioned earlier, one Thanksgiving we brought together and fed ten thousand homeless people at LA's Union Rescue Mission. One man wrote me later and said, "Before I came there, the most choice I had was where I was going to sleep and what garbage can I was going to pull my food out of. After being here one year with no alcohol, no drugs, no sex, I now have ability as a printer, and I've got three job offers, the lowest of which is $40,000 a year." We fed the man, but we also taught the man to feed himself.

My number two goal: house unhoused humanity quickly, safely, and satisfyingly.

My third goal: eradicate illiteracy, first in America and then around the world. My daddy was an illiterate Danish fellow. I loved him, but I now know that illiteracy is the greatest prison.

My fourth goal: to have an interconnecting electrical network all the way around our planet, a goal first set out by Buckminster Fuller. It's supported by the GENI Initiative, spearheaded by the GENI Global Energy Network Institute, founded by my friend Peter Meisen in San Diego.

One of my biggest goals is to reforest the planet with eighteen billion trees, because our parents, out of ignorance and apathy, cut down so many for houses, roads, hospitals, and hotels. I want you to plant three trees. One for being born, one if you ever plan on dying, and one if you've ever fallen in love with somebody. I want people to plant fruit trees so the homeless and hungry will have something good and nourishing to eat. Inspire everyone to plant fruit trees, and our world will be more of a Garden of Eden. I want to discover all the herbs for healing on our planet.

The Power of Mentoring

One of the most efficient ways to get to the end from beginning is have a mentor, a great and inspiring teacher.

François Fénelon, the archbishop of Cambrai, France, during the reign of Louis XIV, penned letters that were collected into a book called *Let Go*. In it he wrote, "Self is the only prison that can bind the soul." As archbishop, Fénelon became the spiritual advisor of a small number of earnest people who sought to live a life of true spirituality in the midst of a court that was shamelessly immoral. During this association with these people, he had many opportunities to write, encouraging them to press toward the goal of Christian perfection.

I had an opportunity to study with one of the wise mentors at Southern Illinois University (SIU) in Carbondale, Illinois. It was here that I first heard Dr. R. Buckminster Fuller, chairman emeritus of the design department.

I was mesmerized by him. I had never heard anyone who was so wise, so important, so world-changing as Fuller. At seventy-one, he stood a little over five feet tall, had close-cropped white hair, and had an aura that glowed as the stage lights hit his glasses. He was strong and athletic-looking and carried himself with distinguished grace and aplomb.

Fuller's message was that youth would be changing the world with computer technology, which he called "education automation in great thinking." He urged us each to reawaken our inner genius.

Here are some of Bucky's suggestions for benefitting from a mentor.

1. **Get a mentor.** Get up close and personal with a mentor. Carry their suitcases, chauffeur them. Do whatever it takes to be in service to them.

2. **Learn your mentor's body of knowledge.** Listen with an inner and an outer ear to what they're saying, doing, and being.

3. **Take copious notes of what your mentor says.** Ask yourself, what am I learning? How can I use this in the future? What should I ask? What should I do? What do these ideas really mean? Can I apply them in my life now and in the future? How can I use their meaning to grow my success?

4. **Learn all that your mentor knows and will teach you.** Read everything he or she has read, recommended, and written. Become a student of your mentor. Alexander the Great learned from Aristotle; Plato learned from Socrates. I don't believe you'll find anyone truly great that doesn't acknowledge his or her mentor's roles in their life. Learn all that the mentor has to share and get next to them. Make their network your network, and understand that there's going to be a lifelong process as you go from mentor to mentor.

Dr. Alfred Richardson at SIU brought me to hear Dr. Fuller. It was like being in the dark cave Plato talks about and then being taken out into the light of day. At first, you'll squint to take in a little gradually, progressively. You open your eyes and learn the traits of your big-thinking mentor. Then you become the mentor: each one teach one, and each one reach one is the cliché in the street.

The Inventor of the Pacemaker

At one point, we were doing a book called *Chicken Soup for the Hawaiian Soul*. The lady who was writing it with us said, "You've got to meet this guy who lives in Kona. He's one of your neighbors, and I'll bet you're going to love his house."

If you've ever been to Kona, Hawaii, you know it's on the big island, which has eleven of the thirteen climate zones. Kona is the desert side. I have a second home there, and love it.

As you drive out past Kona International Airport, there's a place where the road goes inland and you can look down to the sea. There's an exquisitely beautiful estate on the blue Pacific Ocean, which is always glistening turquoise.

I'd always wondered how to get there because there's no road access. All of sudden, I was going to this house with my colleague. It was owned by the late Dr. Earl Bakken.

We went down a dirt road where the rocks removed, as if we were going into Batman's cave. Because it was a hot day, the car windows were down, and I could hear music playing. I asked my colleague, "What is that?"

"When he was in New Zealand," she said, "Dr. Bakken learned that if you play music, crops grown 25 to 75 percent faster."

When we got up in front of Dr. Bakken's manse, he had the biggest amethyst geode I'd ever seen. Amethyst absorbs negative energy, only allowing positive energy in. Dr. Bakken was into feng shui, so he had all the ley lines in his house right, with the doors exactly at the right place. The house was enveloped in beautiful tropical flowers.

Dr. Bakken greeted us at the door and welcomed us in. As we walked in, the first thing I saw was a two thousand-square-foot, triple-cushioned dance floor. Dr. Bakken and his wife, then in their seventies, danced two hours every night for exercise.

We got to spend a few hours together. It was enlightening, because Dr. Earl Bakken was an inventor of the heart pacemaker valves and founder of Medtronic, a company in the Minneapolis area. Earl and one other man started out to create an implantable transistor pacemaker with valves. At first, none of the doctors wanted it. They thought that it was dumbest idea ever. But the pacemaker worked. This invention kept my dad alive for twenty-three years longer than he would have lived without it. I almost wanted to kiss Dr. Bakken out of gratitude.

Today Medtronic has over ninety thousand employees and helps seventy-two million people a year, according to the company's website.

Dr. Bakken created hundreds of implantable devices for both cardiology and neurology, improving the quality as well as the length of life for sufferers of diseases like Parkinson's disease and spastic cerebral palsy.

When you read about these great innovators, you discover a crucial insight: beginnings and endings are fluid. You can see the end in sight now. Go into your deepest, innermost, highest state of consciousness, and decorate the home entertainment center that is your mind with ends that are going to be your new beginnings.

12

Camelot Realized

Camelot comes to us through the British legends of King Arthur, who wanted to create an ideal spot where people could live happily ever after. You can experience Camelot realized. This means that you're living your ideal life right here and right now. As you do, your Camelot can change the world.

Camelot realized is different for each of us. I believe you've been encoded in your DNA and RNA with some tasks, some life assignment, an inner purpose that, if realized, will take us one step closer to Camelot individually and collectively.

Start figuring out what your Camelot is. Ask yourself some questions on paper and write down the answers. Just let it flow. Here are some starter questions:

What makes me happiest?

What's my right livelihood?

Who am I?

What do I need to do to be happy, healthy, prosperous, successful, peaceful, and joyous?

What would the wisest person alive do to solve the problem I have now?

Sometimes our personal Camelot arrives initially as a tragedy. We need to convert all personal tragedies into triumphs. I've already mentioned stories that attest to this possibility. Jana Stanfield's tragic auto accident was her wakeup call to move out of where she was to where she wanted to be—writing, talking, creating, and performing magical inspirational music, which moves people's hearts and souls.

My own wakeup call was a 1974 bankruptcy, where I took something tragic and made it into something magic. Trying to be Buckminster Fuller rather than a really good Mark Victor Hansen, I was building $2 million a year worth of business with Bucky's invention: geodesic domes made out of plastic polyvinyl chloride. When the oil embargo hit in 1974, we couldn't get the raw materials anymore. I went bankrupt so fast that I checked a book out of the library entitled *How to Go Bankrupt by Yourself.* I was in the pits for a long time, but then all of a sudden, from listening to the tape by Cavett Robert, as I've said, I got it. What I really wanted to do—and I'd had this vision since I was sixteen—was to talk to people about things that matter in order to make a life changing difference. Originally, I was a speaker that wrote, and now I'm a writer that speaks. Retrospectively, I can say that my bankruptcy was my best worst experience, although I don't recommend that you go through the same thing.

Throughout these chapters, I've asked you to come back from your future. Ask yourself, what do you want to be remembered for a hundred years from today? Have you written a hundred-year plan, complete with a memorable legacy? What's out ten years from now? Come back from your future. Peter J. Daniels invested days in praying, meditating, and visualizing his progress from metaphorical rags to riches. He visualized himself in five- and ten-year chunks. He saw them in terms of the growth of his kids, which made it easy for him to understand where he'd be at different times. Paul J. Meyer visualized his future as giving away a billion dollars in his lifetime. If you've never decided to be a masterful giver, think about it, because life gives to giver and takes from the taker; if you study Paul's life, you'll see that it works. The possibilities for your Camelot are endless if you visualize them back from the future.

Jim Rohn has wisely said, "Don't start a day until you finish it. Don't start a week until you finish it. Don't start a year until you finish it. Likewise, don't start your next ten years, or hundred years, until you've finished them." You're trading your life for something: make it something wonderful, cherishable, something that makes a significant difference, so you'll look back on your life and say it was well lived. Are you investing in your life and making it worthwhile to you?

Seed Thinking

The thing I feel coded to do at the level of my DNA and RNA is refreshing our planet quickly, safely, and satisfyingly by planting eighteen billion trees. Doing so is going to stop global warming, purify the air, heal the planet, and make it more beautiful. I've asked you to plant trees bearing edible organic fruit, and use the excess growth to feed the hungry.

Just think: an apple tree only bears a few pieces of fruit, but by the tenth year, it delivers over ten thousand apples. Bob Schuller used to say that anyone can count the seeds in an apple, but only God can count the apples in a seed.

Use that kind of seed thinking here. Understand that there's more than enough for everyone, and let's make this earth more like the Garden of Eden, which, in my mind, is Camelot realized. The Garden of Eden is here and now if we bring it up-to-date. If we can get it inside our minds, we can get it outside in our experience.

One year, Jack and I and our publisher gifted the earth with a quarter million trees, planted at Yellowstone National Park. We worked with the Arbor Foundation from Nebraska. As writers and printers of books, we wanted to show responsibility for reforesting what we'd used up.

We challenge everyone everywhere in the publishing business to do likewise—publishers of books, magazines, news periodicals, anyone who uses paper. That probably includes you.

Be about your father's business. Be about reforesting our planet. Why not give your kids, grandkids and great-grandkids good, clean, fresh air to breathe? Why not give them a planet that doesn't overheat and whose icecaps don't melt? Let's reforest the planet. Agree with me, and then we'll have two minds agreeing. We'll just make it so.

Werner Erhard, creator of the EST seminars and the Hunger Project, taught that if enough of us visualize the end of hunger, it would and could happen. John F. Kennedy garnered enough focus, energy, and belief to land a man on the moon, not in ten years, which was his original goal, but in eight years and two months. The Maharishi Mahesh Yoga got his transcendental meditators to concentrate their energy in order to push back crime and violence in some local areas for specific periods of time. Perhaps if we could focus enough energy, we could banish fear, violence, and crime, at least temporarily.

Changing the World, One Story at a Time

Earlier I shared some of my hundred-year goals with you. Jack and I and our Chicken Soup for the Soul team want to change the world one story at a time. Hopefully, you'll share some of our stories, and it'll stimulate you to share your stories and get others to share theirs. Let's get the whole world communicating.

Storytelling will heal lots of wounds. In *Chicken Soup for the Soul Two*, we tell an anecdote from the Jewish philosopher Martin Buber, whose grandfather was lame. Martin's grandfather was once asked to tell a story about his teacher and related how his teacher used to hop and dance while he prayed. During his storytelling, his grandfather was so swept away by the story that he began to hop and dance to show how his teacher had done it. From that same hour, he was cured of his lameness.

In my version of Camelot, storytelling constitutes a form of good medicine called *psychoneuroimmunology*. That's *psycho*, meaning *mind*, *neuro*, meaning *nerves*, and *immunology*, relating to the immune system.

Diana Nightingale, the widow of the late Earl Nightingale, called and told us her story. Diana had a gut-wrenching flu. She read one of our books cover to cover in three hours. The stories galvanized her spirit and healed her. Our words, read by Diana, brought her spirit and body back to wellness and wholeness.

The Bible says your words have the power to curse or bless, give life or death. Allow me to paraphrase: your words can make you healthy, and they can also make you seriously sick.

For me now, Camelot realized is creating and sharing great ideas, great thinking, and great love. I love creating, writing, adding to, and editing the script. I've shared it with some of the finest minds alive—my friends. I've asked for feedback and feed-forward. I want ideas and criticism.

Years ago, our friend Dr. Ken Blanchard, author of *The One Minute Manager*, told Jack and me at breakfast, "Feedback is the breakfast of champions." I want this book to be the best I'm capable of at this moment. Simultaneously, I'm creating multiple other extraordinary books and programs that titillate me at the core of my being. I hope you'll learn vastly from each of them.

Hopefully, you'll love this book so much that you'll share it with others. I'll keep gathering more ideas that thrill and enchant me, and I think will do the same for you. My mind is rocking. I'm kicking. I'm amazed how great ideas gush in and gush out.

In business you're either leading-edge, cutting-edge, dull-edge or trailing-edge, and I want you to stay leading-edge.

The late Lee Kuan Yew, former prime minster of the city-state of Singapore from 1959 to 1990, transformed a nation and a people. Lee raised the educational level of his country so that as of 2017, it had a literacy rate of over 97 percent. Where there were no gardens, he made a desert bloom, an idea he brought home from the flowered boulevards of Paris. He called Singapore the garden city of the world.

Paradise in Your Mind

Let's start thinking of how we can make our entire planet a Garden of Eden. I don't think of the Garden of Eden as having existed six thousand years ago; I think it's in our minds. This is what we're teaching here. The metaphysics of thinking big is the law of correspondence. The outside is always just a reflection of what's going inside your mind. If we start to believe it, we start to achieve it, and it starts to become so. I know it works.

Camelot is a paradise in your mind, composed of hopes and dreams growing out of your experience, and when you get paradise in your mind, you get paradise in your experience. As I've suggested, each of us has coded in our DNA and RNA a dream to participate in the creation of Camelot. Some of us have anesthetized ourselves and forgotten our dreams, desires, and destinies. That doesn't mean they're not there; rather, they're merely sleeping and awaiting the requisite stimulus.

Allow these ideas to be that stimulus. I want to be the gadfly that stabs your spirit alive. I want you to be so alive that you share this book with at least one other person and together you'll help awaken the world. Writer Helen Kromer said, "One mind awake can awaken another. The second awake can awaken their next door brother. Three awake can awaken the town by turning the whole place upside down. Many awake can make such a fuss that they finally awaken the rest of us."

I want you to create your individual Camelot, which will be so exciting you wouldn't trade your life for anything or anyone or choose to live or be anywhere else. I was once asked to help a presidential wannabe. He offered me an ambassadorship to any country in the world that I wanted. I said, "Listen, I appreciate what you're offering, but I just want to be me." I really love speaking, writing, promoting, marketing, thinking, and entrepreneurship.

Your job is to make the ideal real. Everyone has a dream. Sometimes they are hidden in the subterranean layer of our subconscious minds. We want something, but we don't know we want it until we see it, hear it, read it, or dream about it, and our minds are triggered by somebody else's dreams. That's why I suggest you have a dream team with whom you can weekly discuss your dreams, goals, and problems openly, candidly, and confidently.

You say, "I know who I am. I'm Bob or Bernadette." Bunk. You're so much more. You're a spiritual being having a physical experience. You say, "I know what I want."

Bunk. Most of us are babes in our awareness of what we want. We are unlimited. Our supply is truly unlimited.

When I was seven years old I saw my first Sears mail-order catalogue. I was in awe and wonder. I didn't know so many things existed in the whole world. I spent days dreaming and hoping that someday I could buy goodies by mail myself. Little did I know that the Internet was coming and that my supply would multiply almost infinitely.

You say you know where you're going? You really can go anywhere today. When will you get there and whom will you take? First, decide that you want to go to the metaphorical Camelot. Your subconscious can make the provision if you make the decision.

Look at Columbus. When he left, he didn't know where he was going. When he got there, he didn't know where he was. When he got back, he didn't where he'd been, yet in his own inimitable way, he sought and found Camelot. As for who will go with you, they'll show up. Watch the inspiring movie about Christopher Columbus, called *The Discovery*, with Tom Selleck. You'll see that there are those in your immediate vicinity who want somebody to dream a great and inspiring dream and let them share the trip.

Of course, new people will keep emerging in the set called your life, although, as I've already pointed out, most of them will be walk-ons. Be like Michelangelo. Chip out everything that's not in the master template of your mind. Chip out the junk, the weeds, the negativity.

Release your imprisoned splendor; release how you want to be. It's easy then to carve out the imperfections, or at least minimize them, and release that gorgeous, bountiful splendor within.

You and I and everyone are masterpieces in progress. Our goal is daily progress, not perfection. We are merely moving towards our respective Camelots. When one of us gets his or her Camelot, all of us are closer to ours.

The world awaits you with activities that will excite, delight, and ignite your most compelling, adventurous spirit. The cliché says that the world is your oyster. That is true. The oyster creates a pearl when a grain of sand gets in and irritates it to create a thing of beauty. You probably have plenty of irritations that you can now look at in a new light. You can use them to create pearls of great price that will provide you with magnificent new experiences. Why not you? Why not now? Why not here?

The Mistake of Mortality

Let me conclude with a thought-provoking dialogue between King Arthur and the wizard Merlin from Deepak Chopra's book *The Way of the Wizard*. Please read this with an open heart and an awakened belief system.

To unravel this paradox one has to understand time as a wizard experiences it. "You mortals take your name from death," says Merlin in his crystal cave. "You would be called immortals if you believed in yourself as creatures of life."

"That's not fair," Arthur protested. "We didn't choose death; it was thrust upon us."

"No, you are simply used to it. All of you grow old and die because you see others grow old and die. Throw off this worn-out habit, and you will no longer be trapped in the net of time."

"Throw off death? How does one do that?" Arthur wanted to know.

"To begin with, go back to the source of your habit. There you'll find some bit of false reasoning that convinced you to be mortal in the first place. False reasoning lies at the root of any false belief. Then find the flaw in your logic; pluck it out. It is all very simple."

Arthur passed into legend as "the once and future king," implying that he too had escaped the spell of death. What did he find? What is the false logic that wizards see behind mortality? Essentially, it is our identification with the body. Human bodies are born, grow old, and die. Identifying with this process is a false logic, but, once embraced, dooms us to die as well. We fall under the spell of mortality and have no choice but to embrace death.

To break the spell requires a shift of identity from being timebound to being timeless. Therefore the wizard sets out on a journey to discover the truth about time—this is the real meaning behind the tale of Merlin, who lived backwards in time. He wanted to follow time back to its roots.

How do we buy out of the belief in death and reconceptualize ourselves as immortals rather than mortals, living in timelessness rather than in fragmented, timebound awareness?

What if Chopra is right, and we have misnamed ourselves as mere mortals? The Bible says our words have the power to curse or to bless, to cause life or death. What if we reprogram ourselves to believe in our own immortality? Anthropologist Margaret Mead said, "Never doubt that a small group of thoughtful, committed citizens can change the world; indeed, it's the only thing that ever has."

I'll bet you agree. I ask you to read this book twenty-one times, take ownership of these ideas, and share them with like-minded friends. Let's realize Camelot together.

Let's Talk Story

In Hawaii, people live longer than anywhere else in America. Their longevity is attributed to the idyllic trade winds, scented, warm, tropical breezes, perfect weather, clean air, and relaxed lifestyle.

I think two more things are involved. First, Hawaiians like to say, "Let's talk story." They still gather together with friends and family just to converse. Psychiatrists tell us we'll go crazy if we don't talk and share our feelings and our love, animation, and emotion.

Second, in Hawaii there is still *ohana*—the family, the basis of social organization, family dinners, luaus, being together. If you don't have *ohana*, create one. Realize your own perfect Camelot family. Many others no longer want to be lonely either. People can join, befriend, and find each other beloved. If you have an *ohana*, bring in a lost soul now and then, and embrace the aloha spirit of love, togetherness, and joy of being.

Fully express who you really are. You've learned you're a genius and can apply your wisdom. The more you use wisdom and genius, the more you'll have to use. It's an inexhaustible supply. The source is infinite.

You've now been taught to plug into God—infinite intelligence or, as the theologian Pierre Teilhard de Chardin called it, the noosphere. It's there for the asking. Think big, ask big, act big, live big, earn big, save big. Dedicate yourself not just to a little Camelot for you, but to the big Camelot for everyone, everywhere. It doesn't cost any more. Just think a little bit bigger.

Merlin advised, "Ponder not what you see, Arthur, but why you see it." Think not from your limited self but from your unlimited self. Visualize from your divinity, not from your humanity. Take God's eyes and look through your heart, soul, and spirit. Infinite wisdom and awareness are yours if you desire and seek them. A true wizard or seer comes as standard operating equipment in each and every one of us. It's automatically installed. All you've got to do is uncover it.

Didn't Jesus say, "He that believeth on me, the works that I do shall he do also; and greater works than these shall he do" (John 14:12)? Listen to your inner voice, and it will say, "Find me. I've always been here, continuously waiting for you. Welcome home. I'm yours to use."

Now to help you get there, I'm going to give you one more movie recommendation. I want you to watch *Camelot*, with Richard Harris and Vanessa Redgrave. I've watched it multiple times, and it moves my soul and being. The music is commanding and lives hauntingly in the mind.

I'm hoping that you'll get to live in a Camelot; I believe there was such a place. You and I can cherish the vision of Camelot, where violence is not strength and compassion is not weakness, where love is to be expanded, shared, and enjoyed—a Garden of Eden that can be wrapped around our whole spaceship earth, making it healthy, happy, and whole for human, plant, and animal life. Where everyone gets to have his or her day in the sun, because there's more than enough sun for everyone. Where peace can reign and solutions can be found to problems. In Camelot realized, we create and live happily every after.

That finishes this book. I think that you realize your Camelot and I realize mine in order to take care of people who haven't had the chance to realize theirs.

With that I say, "Blessings on you for reading this, and I hope your blessings have blessings as you realize Camelot and think bigger than you ever thought you could."

CPSIA information can be obtained
at www.ICGtesting.com
Printed in the USA
JSHW050942310521
15358JS00002B/2